Supply Chain Collaboration

How to Implement CPFR® and Other Best Collaborative Practices

by
Ronald K. Ireland with Colleen Crum

THE EDUCATIONAL SOCIETY
FOR RESOURCE MANAGEMENT

Copyright ©2005 by J. Ross Publishing, Inc.

ISBN 1-932159-16-9

Printed and bound in the U.S.A. Printed on acid-free paper
10 9 8 7 6 5 4 3 2 1

Library of Congress Cataloging-in-Publication Data

Ireland, Ronald, 1952-
    Supply chain collaboration : how to implement CPFR and other best
collaborative practices / by Ronald Ireland with Colleen Crum.
        p.   cm.
    "CPFR" in subtitle is followed by the registered trademark symbol.
    ISBN 1-932159-16-9 (hardback : alk. paper)
    1. Business logistics. I. Crum, Colleen, 1953- II. Title.
        HD38.5.I74 2005
        658.7—dc22   2004026583

CPFR® is a Registered Trademark of the Voluntary Interindustry Commerce Standards
(VICS) Association.

Direct all inquiries to J. Ross Publishing, Inc., 6501 Park of Commerce Blvd., Suite 200, Boca Raton, Florida 33487.

Phone: (561) 869-3900
Fax: (561) 892-0700
Web: www.jrosspub.com

DEDICATION

To my loving wife, Mary, and my wonderful children, Kevin and Amy,
who have been the foundation and joy in my life.
And to my father, Keith Ireland, a retired cookie salesman,
who taught me the common sense concepts of supply chain collaboration
and the importance of taking care of the customer.

—Ronald K. Ireland

TABLE OF CONTENTS

FOREWORD

Collaboration — easier said than done, but mission critical in today's increasingly demanding business environment. Successful companies of tomorrow will be those that drive the use of supply chain collaboration more strategically, creating new revenue opportunities, efficiencies, and customer loyalty. Collaborative commerce will be the defining business discipline of the twenty-first century.

Supply chain collaboration is truly a transformational business strategy that will have a profound effect on competitive success. This is because the new economy is founded on the forces of new technologies and the increasing importance of intangible assets such as relationships and knowledge.

The model for creating value has changed. Today, companies have highly desegregated value chains, where the majority of operational efficiencies and revenue-enhancement opportunities can only come from greater visibility, integration, and synchronization among companies in a value network. Collaboration outside the physical walls of the enterprise is the new arena for value creation.

This, in turn, is powering revolutionary new value propositions that delight customers while delivering exceptional economics and sustainable differentiation to the innovator. Today's industry leaders, companies like Dell, Cisco, and Wal-Mart, are driving the use of supply chain collaboration enabled by technology to transform their supply chains, delivering differentiated capability, value, and competitive advantage in the process.

The book you are holding provides a comprehensive "how to" guide to supply chain collaboration, whether you are just beginning the journey or moving from pilot to implementation. It is a unique and valuable compilation of important learnings and best practices to help you avoid the pitfalls and accelerate the entire implementation process. As one of the early supply chain collaboration pioneers who collected a few arrows in the back on the path to victory, I can attest to its value!

While the techniques covered here can deliver almost immediate bottom-line results, the bigger idea is to use supply chain collaboration as a catalyst for change, a transformational strategy to create new business models.

A foundation principle of supply chain management is that significant leverage can be obtained by working with suppliers and customers as if they were part of an integrated, seamless pipeline. Enabled with today's technology, the dream of supply chain transparency and real-time interaction with all trading partners has become a reality capable of producing unprecedented, seamless, and continuous exchanges across the supply chain.

Significant efficiencies can be gained by linking the supply chain and removing unnecessary inventory, variation, cost, and reducing cycle times to create an "extended enterprise." In an extended enterprise environment, the sharing of information leads to commonality of goals, increased velocity of trade, and meshing of business processes. With this more robust, collaborative commerce platform, the emphasis shifts from simply connecting partners (mostly transaction oriented) to coordinating interbusiness processes. This is key because coordination is more knowledge and process oriented and synchronization at this level creates more value across the chain. Case in point, the entire "lean" management concept depends on input from all links in the value chain to function successfully.

Collaboration occurs when companies work together for mutual benefit. It means they leverage each other on an operational basis so that together they perform better than they could separately. Collaboration can occur all along the value chain, from design collaboration through procurement to final distribution. This allows companies that share information to shorten processing time dramatically, eliminate value-depleting activities, and improve quality, accuracy, and asset productivity.

Supply chain collaboration and creating an "extended enterprise" offer dramatic improvement in performance, but also demand radical changes in thinking and behavior. There is no silver bullet. The key is good business process integration and customer focus. This requires clearly identifying consumer value, thinking externally, and viewing your supply chain as a strategic differentiator.

Welcome to the path forward in the twenty-first century!

> *Ralph W. Drayer, Founder and Chairman*
> *Supply Chain Insights LLC and*
> *Former Chief Logistics Officer,*
> *The Procter & Gamble Company*

ACKNOWLEDGMENTS

Ronald K. Ireland

As a practitioner for over twenty-five years in supply chain processes, I have had the privilege of working closely with many thought leaders from different industries. I have been blessed with the privilege of associating with the "Who's Who" of supply chain visionaries and for that I am most thankful.

With this in mind, the writing of this book is a collaboration of my first-hand experiences with many of these great people and companies.

I first would like to thank the team of Oliver Wight Americas, who I first met in the late 1980s when I was involved in a major manufacturing resource planning effort at Martin Marietta Aerospace (now part of Lockheed Martin). It was there that I was first introduced to the Proven Path as well as the consulting model of using only the best subject matter experts in the industry. The guidance that was provided through education, knowledge transfer, and a proven methodology was amazing to observe and be a part of. So special thanks for this great experience to Roger Brooks and his team of Oliver Wight consultants, as well as to the Martin Marietta team led by Mickey Clemons and Cliff Whisenhunt.

After departing Martin Marietta, I was fortunate enough to work for Wal-Mart Stores, Inc., where I had the privilege of working with some of the greatest supply chain thought leaders I have ever been associated with. It was while I was at Wal-Mart that the concept of supply chain collaboration, as described in this book, was first created. Special thanks go to Robert Bruce, who is truly one of the greatest visionaries of supply chain collaboration. I appreciate his assistance in writing Chapter 3 about Wal-Mart's success. Also special thanks to Randy Mott, Rick Dalzell, Randy Salley, David Ferrell, Melissa Turner, Mike Casey, Terry Davis, Tom DeMott, Bobbie Aldridge, Chrys Tarvin, and Larry Fennel, as well as to the Wal-Mart forecasting and replenishment team, for their visionary ideas that led to many of the supply chain concepts and architecture used in today's collaborative best practices.

It was during my time at Wal-Mart that we designed and executed the first pilot on supply chain collaboration, called CFAR (Collaborative Forecasting and Replenishment). This successful pilot led to the development of today's supply chain collaboration industry standard, CPFR® (Collaborative Planning, Forecasting, and Replenishment), that is sponsored by VICS (the Voluntary Interindustry Commerce Standards Association, Inc.). The people involved with CFAR and CPFR® are the true heroes in establishing today's supply chain collaborative best practices.

Special thanks go to the team at Warner-Lambert, Jay Nearnberg and Bob Uccardi, as well as to the other CFAR team members, including Maggie Gynum of SAP, Dawn Andre of Manugistics, and Jim Uchneat and Ted Rybeck of Benchmarking Partners. I also am greatly indebted to Jay Nearnberg for his assistance and insights in writing Chapter 4 on Warner-Lambert's success.

CPFR® would not be where it is today without the great leadership that Joe Andraski has provided for the VICS CPFR® Working Group. The CPFR® Working Group has many volunteer heroes from the many companies that actively participate in the organization. Special acknowledgment for their contributions goes to Jim McLaughlin, Jean Schenck, Laura Golding, Larry Roth, Chuck Rehlin, Fred Baumann, Matt Johnson, Ron Burnette, Andrew Wight, Andrew Hern, and Jack Haedicke. Special thanks also to Fred Baumann of JDA, Matt Johnson of Syncra, and Dirk Kansky of SAP for their help in writing the technology overview in Chapter 8.

I also would like to add a special thanks to Anne Hilton for helping to edit this book, Stephanie Willett and Jill Losik for help on the graphics, and Susan Hansen for her efforts in coordinating the book's development.

I cannot do justice to all of the people I have been associated with and apologize to those of you I have failed to mention. The concept of supply chain collaboration has evolved from the hard work of thousands of leading thought leaders. I thank all of you for your drive to push all industries toward collaborative partnerships.

Finally, I want to give my special thanks to my co-author, Colleen "Coco" Crum. Her enthusiasm and thought-provoking leadership are contagious. I am honored that she is a part of writing this book and assisting in driving all industries toward supply chain collaboration.

Colleen Crum

New business models can take decades to take hold and attain critical mass. This has been the case with supply chain collaboration.

Some people express frustration with the length of time it has taken for companies to embrace supply chain collaboration. Why is it that more executives do not recognize the benefits from collaborating with their trading partners? I believe that they recognize the benefits, but question the time, human resources, and money it will take to implement supply chain collaboration. This book provides a practical "how-to" implementation guide, based largely on Ron Ireland's experience with Wal-Mart and other retailers and consumer goods companies.

In working with Ron to develop this book, I was drawn back to the mid-1990s and the effort of the Canadian grocery industry to define continuous replenishment models. Like their counterparts in the United States, these early pioneers saw that collaborating with supply chain partners would strip waste from the supply chain and bring profits to all supply chain partners. They did not just study these models, however; they put them to use — and that is a key lesson learned.

Many companies have been waiting for the "perfect" model, supported by "perfect" software. In doing so, they miss out on the financial benefits that can be derived *today* from implementing supply chain collaboration.

I dedicate this book to the supply chain collaboration practitioners who are pioneering a new way of doing business. I thank Daphne Perry, formerly of H.J. Heinz of Canada, and Dale Ross, of Effem Foods, for their generosity in exposing me to the concepts of supply chain partnering and the practicalities of making it work. I salute my clients for their efforts to improve financial and operational performance and my colleagues at The Oliver Wight Companies for helping them to do so.

Finally, I am grateful for the opportunity to collaborate with and learn from Ron Ireland.

ABOUT THE AUTHORS

Ronald K. Ireland, a managing principal with Oliver Wight Americas, is a globally recognized visionary to many of today's value chain best practices. He has over twenty-five years of business process and technology experience with leading companies, with a primary focus in demand and supply chain processes for retail, manufacturing, technology, and aerospace. Six of those years of experience were specific to the area of strategic consulting at the executive level.

Ron's manufacturing experience at Martin Marietta included technology responsibility for projects that achieved six Class A MRPII implementations. He then led a technology staff on software development projects for store and warehouse replenishment, forecasting, supply chain collaboration, procurement, micromerchandising, labor scheduling, and data mining for Wal-Mart Stores, Inc., one of the world's leading retail chains. While Ron was with Wal-Mart, he was presented several awards. One of the awards that Ron received was for "Technology Visionary of The Year — 1995." This award was presented for Ron's design and implementation of Wal-Mart Replenishment Planning (WRP), which included the concept of supply chain collaboration. This design and proof of concept pilot led to the creation of CPFR® (Collaborative Planning, Forecasting, and Replenishment).

Ron was a Director with J.D. Edwards, a software company, and is now a consultant and educator to companies in retail, consumer goods manufacturing, industrial manufacturing, telecommunications, high technology, grocery, apparel, aerospace, and software development.

Ron has been interviewed by and published in many leading industry publications and is a frequent public speaker at industry conferences and at many leading colleges and universities. He earned his B.S. in business management from Southwest Missouri State University and participated in the Sam Walton Institute in Retail as well as Dale Carnegie.

Colleen Crum is a managing principal with the Oliver Wight Companies. She has assisted many companies in implementing sales and operations planning, demand management, and forecasting.

Colleen has been involved in the food industry's supply chain management effort. She participated in the development of "ECR: Road Map to Continuous Replenishment," published by Canadian food industry trade groups in 1995. The publication documented the best continuous replenishment practices in Canada, addressing logistics, distribution, transportation, and resource planning.

She co-authored (with George Palmatier) the books *Enterprise Sales and Operations Planning* and *Demand Management Best Practices*, published by J. Ross Publishing.

ABOUT APICS

APICS — The Educational Society for Resource Management is a not-for-profit international educational organization recognized as the global leader and premier provider of resource management education and information. APICS is respected throughout the world for its education and professional certification programs. With more than 60,000 individual and corporate members in 20,000 companies worldwide, APICS is dedicated to providing education to improve an organization's bottom line. No matter what your title or need, by tapping into the APICS community you will find the education necessary for success.

APICS is recognized globally as:

- The source of knowledge and expertise for manufacturing and service industries across the entire supply chain
- The leading provider of high-quality, cutting-edge educational programs that advance organizational success in a changing, competitive marketplace
- A successful developer of two internationally recognized certification programs, Certified in Production and Inventory Management (CPIM) and Certified in Integrated Resource Management (CIRM)
- A source of solutions, support, and networking for manufacturing and service professionals

For more information about APICS programs, services, or membership, visit www.apics.org or contact APICS Customer Support at (800) 444-2742 or (703) 354-8851.

Free value-added materials available from
the Download Resource Center at www.jrosspub.com

At J. Ross Publishing we are committed to providing today's professional with practical, hands-on tools that enhance the learning experience and give readers an opportunity to apply what they have learned. That is why we offer free ancillary materials available for download on this book and all participating Web Added Value™ publications. These online resources may include interactive versions of material that appears in the book or supplemental templates, worksheets, models, plans, case studies, proposals, spreadsheets and assessment tools, among other things. Whenever you see the WAV™ symbol in any of our publications, it means bonus materials accompany the book and are available from the Web Added Value Download Resource Center at www.jrosspub.com.

Downloads available for *Supply Chain Collaboration: How to Implement CPFR® and Other Best Collaborative Practices* consist of CPFR® white papers, VICS CPFR® roundtable discussion slides, and a CPFR® readiness assessment grid.

THE LURE OF SUPPLY CHAIN COLLABORATION

Today, economic pressures are forcing companies to alter the way they are doing business. Competition is tougher, and for companies operating in many industries, competition is global. Customers are more demanding and less loyal than ever before and it is harder to make money. Companies cannot simply raise prices to attain profit margin goals and there is not much left to cut from operating costs.

So what is the answer? Companies are increasingly looking beyond their individual enterprises to find ways to increase sales revenue and profit margins. In today's business world, there is an increased focus on the effectiveness of the supply chains. Ineffective supply chains are increasingly being seen as "money pits" that strip enterprises of cash flow when inventory is not needed and sales revenue when product is not available to sell. As a result, new business models are being developed to leverage and improve supply chain performance.

For decades, supply chain competency was defined as an ability to react well. The heroes in companies were often managers adroit enough to ensure that a last-minute order could be reacted to and fulfilled. There was little awareness of the cost of fulfilling that order. Usually, the price a company paid in reacting well was to increase costs in fulfilling the order. The fact that this reduced profit margins in turn was (and still is) often ignored.

Reacting really well in today's business environment is not good enough to survive financially over the long term. When net profit margins range from 5 to 7 percent in the consumer goods industry, 4 to 6 percent in the mass

Retailers' Benefits	Suppliers' Benefits
• Improved products in stock: 2 to 8 percent	• Reduced inventory: 10 to 40 percent
• Reduced inventory: 10 to 40 percent	• Increased replenishment cycles: 12 to 30 percent
• Increased sales: 5 to 20 percent	• Increased sales: 2 to 10 percent
• Reduced logistics costs: 3 to 4 percent	• Improved customer service: 5 to 10 percent

Figure 1.   Benefits of Supply Chain Collaboration.

merchandise retail industry, and 2 to 4 percent in food retail, companies cannot afford a reactive business model. Over the past decade, the efforts of Wal-Mart, Target, Procter & Gamble, Sears, Ace Hardware, Rite Aid, JC Penney, Kimberly-Clark, Cisco Systems, and Dell Computer have shown that an anticipatory business model is better able to increase sales revenues and deliver profit margins that shareholders expect. Anticipation requires cooperation and collaboration among all partners within a supply chain. That is what this book is about.

When discussing how to better cooperate and collaborate with supply chain partners, it is not uncommon for executives to ask: What will be the financial benefit? This is a legitimate question. Migrating to an anticipatory model that involves cooperation and collaboration with supply chain partners requires an investment in skills and competence, process development, and technology. Executives rightly ask: Will it be worth the effort to adopt this new business model?

AMR Research published study findings on the financial benefits of CPFR® (Collaborative Planning, Forecasting, and Replenishment), which is what the retail and consumer packaged goods industries call supply chain partnering programs. Figure 1 shows the financial benefits cited in this study of ninety-four companies.*

One of the interesting findings of this study is the fact that companies that collaborate effectively simultaneously increase sales revenue while they also significantly reduce operating expenses. These results are drawing the attention of many corporate executives. The line of thought has shifted from "What is the hoopla about collaboration all about?" to "What could supply chain collaboration do for our company and how do we get started?"

To get started answering this question, consider the benefits cited in the AMR Research study. If your company achieved the minimum benefits cited, what would be the quantitative benefit? Figure 2 provides a roadmap worksheet

---

* Suleski, Janet, Beyond CPFR: Retail Collaboration Comes of Age, AMR Research Report, April 1, 2001.

Retailers' Benefits According to AMR Research Study	*If You Are a Retailer, Quantify the Financial Benefit if Your Company Achieved the Minimum Benefit Cited in the AMR Research Study*
• Improved products in stock: 2 to 8 percent	
• Reduced inventory: 10 to 40 percent	
• Increased sales: 5 to 20 percent	
• Reduced logistics costs: 3 to 4 percent	

Suppliers' Benefits According to AMR Research Study	*If You Are a Retailer, Quantify the Financial Benefit if Your Company Achieved the Minimum Benefit Cited in the AMR Research Study*
• Reduced inventory: 10 to 40 percent	
• Increased replenishment cycles: 12 to 30 percent	
• Increased sales: 2 to 10 percent	
• Improved customer service: 5 to 10 percent	

Figure 2.   Roadmap 1: Calculating Benefits from Supply Chain Collaboration.

to help you document the potential benefit. Throughout this book, you will find similar roadmap worksheets.

As companies begin to realize the potential financial benefit from supply chain partnering, executives are increasingly thinking of supply chain collaboration as a corporate transformational strategy. Executives are asking what is needed to implement this transformational strategy successfully. This, in turn, is causing executives to examine how to best develop and enable people, processes, and technology to support supply chain collaboration.

To learn what it takes to collaborate with supply chain partners successfully, many executives are reaching outside of their own industry to learn what other industries are doing to improve supply chain processes. This is a vast difference from ten years ago when I worked as an information technology manager for Wal-Mart and was assigned the task of developing the company's collaborative capability. We had no one to turn to within the retail industry and very few companies that were thought leaders among our suppliers.

Today, companies operating in high technology, retail, consumer product goods manufacturing, and, most recently, the aerospace and defense industry have industry standards groups as a resource. These groups have formed to document best-practice models and to provide guidance for companies interested in supply chain partnering.* In essence, these groups provide a means to

---

* Three examples of organizations that support supply chain partnering are the Voluntary Interindustry Commerce Standards (VICS) Association, which was initially formed to support the retail industry's collaborative partnering effort; RosettaNet, which has helped to guide the high-technology industry; and the Supply Chain Council, which has a broad reach into the manufacturing and services industries.

collaborate about collaboration and play several valuable roles. They are documenting the financial and operational performance improvements achieved through supply chain partnering in a systematic manner. Through conferences to share experiences, they also are highlighting the need to develop people skills and process competence as well as to utilize appropriate technology to facilitate the trading of partner information.

Information sharing between trading partners is no longer inhibited by the lack of enabling technology as it was in the early 1990s. With the introduction of the Internet and the development of many robust business-to-business (B2B) technology solutions, we now have the tools to adopt scalable and automated information trading in support of collaboration programs. The lack of an automated means for trading information among partners can no longer be used as an excuse for not having the capability to develop supply chain partnerships. Now the impediments are understanding how to develop a supply chain transformational strategy and the willpower and perseverance to do so. This was the primary motivating factor for writing this book.

This book was written to help you minimize the risk and speed up the adoption of successful supply chain collaboration in your company. That is why I emphasize the practical ways to implement supply chain collaboration in this book.

As a pioneer and innovator of supply chain collaboration, I have not developed the techniques for the successful collaboration by myself. This book is a compilation of my experience in working with others as well as observing others implement supply chain partnering. Some of our efforts were highly successful; others were failures. We learned from both, and you do not have to repeat our mistakes.

In reading this book, it is important to remember that it is not a "one size fits all" guide to supply chain collaboration. The most successful supply chain collaboration efforts have had a degree of flexibility in adapting to each partner's capabilities as well as the business environment. Therefore, this book is meant to be a guideline, or a roadmap, that you can customize to fit your company's and your trading partners' needs.

QUESTIONS

1. Why are many companies turning to supply chain collaboration today as one of the solutions to managing a more effective and competitive company?
2. What has been a competency for many companies prior to implementing an effective collaborative process?
3. What does CPFR® stand for?

2

THE BULLWHIP EFFECT AND RESULTING SUPPLY CHAIN COSTS

When you think about it, supply chain collaboration makes plain old common sense. It is all about communicating demand information to trading partners so that they can make product, components, and material available at the proper points in the supply chain when they are needed.

When visibility of this need is not available, each business enterprise must estimate (or forecast) what product will be needed, in what quantity, and when. Lacking precise information, these estimates are usually flawed in the following ways:

■ The estimates result in too much product being produced and shipped.
■ The estimates result in not enough product being produced and shipped.

This phenomenon, as shown in Figure 3, was first described by MIT's Jay Forrester* and has been documented further by Hau L. Lee of Stanford University.**

---

* Forrester, Jay W., *Industrial Dynamics,* Productivity Press, 1961. Andre Martin, a pioneer in distribution resource planning, observes: "Jay Forrester never received the credit he truly deserved. He was indirectly responsible for the development of material requirements planning and distribution resource planning. Jay showed the world that there was a rack and pinion relationship across an industrial supply chain. Amplification took place because of different systems that were not connected and differing business practices, such as ordering policies and end-of-month pushes due to sales incentives."
** Lee, Hau L., Creating value through supply chain integration, *Supply Chain Management Review,* September/October 2000, p. 33.

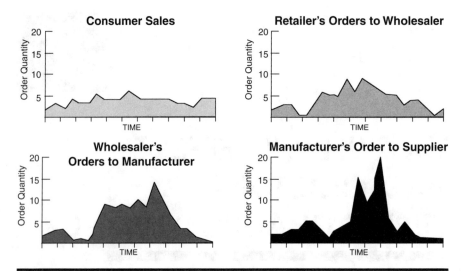

Figure 3. Bullwhip Effect. (©2004 Oliver Wight International.)

When visibility of future demand is lacking, an interesting phenomenon occurs as each partner in the supply chain tries to predict what is needed to support the end user or consumer demand. The business entity closest to the end user or consumer usually has the most precise information of future demand. Those with the business relationship that is the most disconnected from the end user or consumer, such as raw material or component suppliers, usually have the least precise information.

Lacking visibility of true end user or consumer demand, an amplification of the predicted demand is created, as shown in Figure 3. Note how the orders at each point in the supply chain become increasingly different than the actual consumer sales. Note, too, how the manufacturer's orders to the supplier are vastly different from actual consumer sales.

This amplification of demand is most commonly called the bullwhip effect. It is also known by other names, such as:

- Supply chain nervousness
- Supply chain roller coaster effect
- Supply chain tail of the dog

A consequence of the bullwhip effect is supply chain waste — wasted opportunity and wasted money. As you can see from Figure 4, there are times when product that could be sold is unavailable to sell, creating lost or delayed sales revenue. There are also times when there is more inventory than demand,

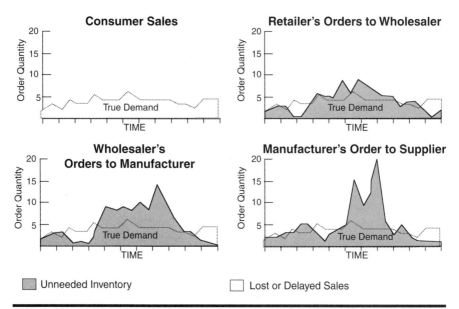

Figure 4. Consequences of the Bullwhip Effect. (©2004 Oliver Wight International.)

which means that valuable resources and cash were wasted on producing product that was not needed.

I and my colleagues, Robert S. Bruce of VCC Associates and Jim Uchneat of Benchmarking Partners, conducted a study to determine the financial impact of the bullwhip effect in the retail industry. The study was based on U.S. Commerce Department statistics. We found that the retail industry carried $1.1 trillion in inventory against retail sales of $3.2 trillion. Simultaneously, the retail industry lost between $7 and $12 billion in sales annually because of out-of-stock situations.*

The financial impact of the bullwhip effect is what is motivating companies to focus on the supply chain. Many companies are developing a supply chain transformation strategy, with supply chain collaboration as a foundation of the strategy. Here is the premise of this strategy: If the demand plans for all supply chain partners more closely resemble anticipated consumer or consumer sales, the cost savings and increased sales opportunities can be very significant.

Without visibility of actual and anticipated demand at the point of consumption, companies are put in the position of having to expend valuable resources unnecessarily in support of what they think, rather than know, will be needed

---

* Ireland, Ron and Bruce, Robert, CPFR: only the beginning of collaboration, *Supply Chain Management Review,* September/October 2000, p. 83.

to support demand. They also must develop highly reactive processes when actual demand materializes differently than the forecast.

In our opinion, you should not confuse reactive with responsive. Some may argue that a reactive process ensures responsiveness to customers, end users, consumers, and the marketplace. But you must ask, at what price? In our view, a responsive process is defined as an anticipatory system that enables each partner in a supply chain to operate in the most cost-effective manner possible to ensure maximum profit.

To develop responsive processes, demand information is needed about the past and future that is as accurate as possible. The most accurate information should come from the business that is closest to the point of consumption. It is the lack of this visibility that compromises companies' ability to ensure that the product, materials, and components are available when they are needed.

There are many reasons why business enterprises in a supply chain are unable to gain visibility of demand information. Some of the reasons are process related; processes are not in place to capture demand history and inputs into a future demand plan. Some of the reasons are information system and tool related; systems and tools are not available to communicate and analyze demand information easily. Some of the reasons are people related; people at all levels of an organization do not have the understanding of why responsive processes are needed. Also, all too often, they have not been trained properly to utilize the process or the systems and tools that support the process.

Figure 5 shows the most common impediments to gaining greater visibility of demand. Note that some of the reasons address internal capabilities. Other reasons are related to a company's ability to interact with its trading partners. You may want to compare your company's current situation with the reasons cited in Figure 5 to see what inhibits your company from gaining greater demand visibility.

Despite best efforts, it is rarely possible to eliminate the bullwhip effect completely. This is caused by ever-changing business dynamics, such as uncertainties about the marketplace, end user and consumer preferences, competition, or other external forces that are difficult to predict with 100 percent accuracy. Also, as we shall see in a moment, mistakes can occur that will amplify the bullwhip effect if not noticed promptly and rectified.

This does not mean that attempts to minimize the bullwhip effect are futile. Consider these results of pilot collaboration efforts that were reported at a VICS CPFR® conference:

■ A 10.3 percent increase in sales for all suppliers of a hardware chain that participated in the collaboration pilot

Impediments to Gaining Visibility of Demand	Does This Impediment Exist in Your Company? (Yes or No)
No formalized demand planning process	
Do not communicate the demand plan to the supply organization so they can communicate plans to suppliers in turn	
No ownership of the demand planning process by the sales and marketing organizations	
Sales and marketing organizations do not provide input into the demand plan	
End of period, quarter, or year sales deals are not communicated	
Poor promotional planning and forecasting	
Forecasts of new item introductions are unreliable	
Unplanned orders from customers	
Ineffective sales and operations planning process to synchronize demand and supply internally	
No or limited visibility of anticipated demand from customers	
No or limited visibility of end user or consumer demand	
Poor demand forecast accuracy	
The forecast or demand plan is not trusted	
Lack of knowledge of customers and their customers' promotion plans	
Do not receive end user or consumer point-of-sale data	
End user or consumer point-of-sale data are received but not considered as input into the demand plan	

Consider this list as a starting point.

Figure 5. Roadmap 2: Impediments to Gaining Visibility of Demand.

- A 5 to 27 percent increase in sales for all suppliers of a grocery chain that participated in the collaboration pilot
- A 12 percent increase in inventory turns for all suppliers of a grocery chain that participated in the collaboration pilot
- A 35 percent reduction in returns to a supplier by a drug store chain
- A $27.6 million reduction in out-of-stock inventory by a retailer

We emphasize that these results were attained from pilot programs, which means that the gains are only the tip of the iceberg. Reducing the bullwhip effect in the supply chain is not the "program or initiative of the month." Rather, it should be a continuous effort. This is a best practice. As one presenter at the VICS CPFR® conference commented: "Don't think of CPFR (Collaborative Planning, Forecasting, and Replenishment) as a replenishment function. Think of it as a supply chain function that impacts all dimensions of the business."*

In continuously working to minimize the bullwhip effect, collaboration with trading partners will evolve. In the early phases of supply chain collaboration, the efforts to minimize the bullwhip effect usually focus on communicating demand information throughout the supply chain. Once greater stability is attained through these efforts, a next phase is to collaborate on promotions.

Experience has shown that there are plenty of opportunities to minimize the bullwhip effect. This takes constant vigilance, communication, and teamwork. Companies think of supply chain collaboration as an automated system or process at their own peril. Here is an example.

When I worked at Wal-Mart as an information technology manager, the information technology group inadvertently created a bullwhip effect. One of the programmers modified a program that drove the creation of replenishment orders for imported merchandise. The changes were minor and the programmer performed all the proper testing. On installing the program, he made one big mistake: the wrong version of the program was installed. This version actually *blocked* purchase orders from being placed. With the purchase orders blocked, the point-of-sale forecasts showed demand volume for imported products going from thousands per week to zero and remaining at zero for the rest of the year. These point-of-sale forecasts were communicated to Wal-Mart's replenishment analysts as well as to suppliers via Retail Link (Wal-Mart's private exchange).

Here is where the collaborative planning process broke down. No one (from Wal-Mart or its suppliers) questioned the change in the point-of-sale forecasts. Plenty of second-guessing occurred, however, with Wal-Mart's suppliers, who made various replenishment and production decisions on their own. This resulted in what we called a large Supply Chain Bullwhip Headache. It took a week before a supplier contacted the Wal-Mart replenishment analyst to verify the forecast.

The moral of this story is: It takes a team approach to eliminate the bullwhip effect. The team members are representatives of companies throughout the supply chain. To perform as a team, team members must be accessible and have

---

* VICS CPFR® Conference, October 2003, Las Vegas, Nevada. Information on the VICS CPFR® organization is available at www.cpfr.org.

developed an openness that encourages communication. Team members also must utilize and review the information that is communicated in a timely manner. And the replenishment system is not a substitute for judgment. These are best practices.

Waiting seven days to question a change in demand (and a dramatic one at that!) is too long. The cause of the bullwhip amplification was a simple technology mistake. The bullwhip amplification resulting from this mistake could have been prevented had there been a regular review of the demand information rather than assuming that the automated replenishment system was always correct. The fact was that these forecasts were generated by an automated replenishment execution system, which means that if the demand forecasts are wrong, so is the replenishment plan. This brings us to another best practice: Supply chain collaboration is not a system; it is a process conducted by people and supported by the system. And the system and people will make mistakes from time to time. A critical element of the process is to prevent mistakes from happening, but when they do happen, to identify and resolve them quickly. This cannot happen if trading partners do not talk with one another.

Case in point: A consumer goods products manufacturing company implemented successful CPFR® pilots with two different major retailers. Once the pilots were operating effectively, the manufacturer decided to hire an hourly employee for each retail account to monitor the retail private exchanges for possible mistakes. Mistakes they wanted to identify early included items being accidentally inactivated, items with the wrong promotional lift, incorrect lead times for items, and incongruencies between store-level demand and the distribution center demand plan.

You may ask: Is it the manufacturer's job to check for errors? The answer is yes and no. You would hope that the retailer could catch its own mistakes, but if the retailer is giving its suppliers free access to its data, why not take advantage of it? Demand and replenishment information provided by retailers creates visibility that is worth a lot of money, as we saw earlier. Receiving this data does not eliminate the need for review and judgment, however, and, yes, error checking.

Another impediment to reducing the bullwhip effect is not using the demand information communicated by trading partners. We call this a failure to internalize trading partner data. This failure understandably frustrates retailers and customers who have invested in the systems and processes to communicate their demand plans, point-of-sale information, and replenishment plans.

What prevents trading partner information from being internalized? All too often, it comes from operating in functional silos. Companies do not recognize the benefit to the entire business enterprise that comes from communicating the customers' and retailers' demand information into the demand planning process and sales and operations planning process.

Customer facing teams are often guilty of hoarding demand information. Customer facing teams are utilized widely in the retail industry. The suppliers to retailers assign teams that typically report to the sales function and work very near to their retailers' corporate headquarters to promote better communication between retailer and supplier. Unfortunately, all too frequently, these teams do not promote communication with their own corporate sales management and planning functions. I have witnessed hundreds of supplier customer facing teams refuse to share any of the retailer data with their own corporate headquarters. These data include point-of-sale information, inventory levels at stores and distribution centers, and demand forecasts.

Why do the customer facing teams not share this valuable information with corporate sales management and demand managers? After all, they are preventing the bullwhip effect from being minimized and it is damaging their company's customer service and financial performance. The reason for not sharing retailer information is usually a misplaced protection of turf.

Many customer facing teams do not trust corporate sales management to support the customer properly and they do not want corporate management questioning the customers' demand plans. The expectation from customer facing teams of their companies often is: React really well, no matter what the cost. As a result, senior executives in companies question the value of supply chain collaboration. Rightfully so, they ask: Where is the win/win? The answer to that question is within the leadership teams of the supplier community.

When customer facing teams are permitted to perform as gatekeepers rather than as communication conduits, ignorance is usually the cause. Throughout the corporation, starting with the senior leaders, people do not understand the impact of not internalizing trading partner information in the company's own planning processes. When trading partner information is not internalized, the following happens.

The corporate demand planning team does not see the customers' demand forecasts, changes in forecasted demand, or planned customer events. Therefore, they use less precise information to develop a demand plan that is communicated to the supply organization. The bullwhip effect is magnified as manufacturing uses this less precise information to communicate schedules to its suppliers, which further amplifies the bullwhip effect and waste in the supply chain. The manufacturer simultaneously ends up with too much inventory of some products and not enough inventory of other products, and probably had to pay overtime and express shipping charges in doing so.

These are self-inflicted wounds that stymie companies from developing a consumer- or end-user-centric focus. It is this focus that helps to minimize the

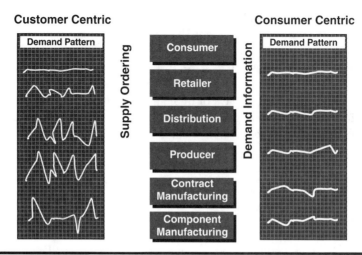

Figure 6.   Customer-Centric Versus Consumer/End-User-Centric Demand Patterns. (©2004 Oliver Wight International.)

bullwhip effect. Increasingly, it is becoming the norm for the retailer or the company closest to the point of consumption to communicate consumer- or end-user-centric demand information. In our opinion, over the next decade, it will become a standard practice for companies closest to the point of consumption to communicate consumer information to their suppliers. It will also become a standard practice for this information to drive the demand plans of their suppliers and all other enterprises that create the supply chain.

It is important to note the difference between consumer centric and customer centric. The consumer is the person who actually buys the products and uses them. The customer may or may not be the consumer. In the case of a retailer, the customer is the consumer. But in the case of a consumer goods manufacturer, the customer is the retailer, and in the case of the raw material provider, the customer is the manufacturer, and so on down each link in the supply chain pipeline.

What has been proven in the academic settings, such as with MIT's beer game,* and confirmed through practical experience is this: When all trading partners have visibility of the consumer or end user demand, the demand can be fulfilled in a more timely and cost-effective manner and inventory can be reduced for all trading partners. In other words, the bullwhip effect is greatly smoothed, as depicted in Figure 6.

---

* Sterman, John D., OR/MS Today, October 1992, MIT Sloan School of Management, Sloan's System Dynamics Group, p. 40.

In working to assist supply chains to reduce the bullwhip effect, I am often reminded that the consumer does not shop in a distribution center. For those manufacturers and their suppliers that have also learned this lesson, their supply chains are not as "nervous." It can be difficult for companies to shift to a consumer-centric view of the business, however.

Case in point: In the early days of implementing supply chain collaboration at Wal-Mart, we struggled to get Procter & Gamble to consider our store-level point-of-sale demand forecast in its demand plans. Procter & Gamble's attention and focus, like most manufacturers, was on Wal-Mart's distribution center orders. The Wal-Mart distribution center was its customer, not the consumer of its products, however. Today, Procter & Gamble is very consumer centric and calls its consumers the "first moment of truth." This is when the consumer stops at the store shelf and decides whether or not to buy Procter & Gamble's products.

Procter & Gamble, one of the pioneers of supply chain collaboration, has reaped the rewards of collaborating with its supply chain partners and of being consumer centric. Industry experts estimate that Procter & Gamble increased sales to Wal-Mart from $350 million in 1998 to $4 billion in 1999 while tripling inventory turns in Wal-Mart stores, as a result of the two companies' collaboration efforts.*

Procter & Gamble, along with other manufacturers like Kraft Foods, Clorox, Conagra, Johnson & Johnson, Gillette, and Kimberly-Clark, recognizes that an accurate demand plan is the key for the manufacturers (and suppliers of the manufacturers) to realize the benefits of supply chain collaboration. And they are increasingly dependent on consumer demand information communicated by their retailers to develop the most accurate demand plan possible.

A great example of how hundreds of manufacturers are quickly realizing the importance of supply chain collaboration and the value of retailer demand information is the building boom going on in Bentonville, Arkansas, the corporate headquarters home of Wal-Mart. While the rest of the United States was experiencing a recession during 2002 and 2003, Bentonville had an unprecedented building boom as hundreds of Wal-Mart vendors constructed large office complexes. Yes, it has been true in the past that vendors often locate local offices close to key customers, but not to the degree that has recently happened at Wal-Mart.

What is different today that makes vendors want to be closer to the retail customer? In the past, vendors primarily only interfaced with the retailer to discuss new promotions or new products or to assist in category management

---

* Robinson, Alan, Is that circle broken, *Food Logistics*, June 15, 1999, p. 48.

activities. Today, major retailers such as Wal-Mart, Target, Sears, Rite Aid, West Marine, Best Buy, and Ace Hardware are sharing so much supply chain collaborative data that the vendors are quickly realizing the value of this information and how they can quickly improve supply chain processing and, most importantly, profits. Having supply chain collaborative teams close to the customer can get the results they desire implemented quickly.

These early adopters of supply chain collaboration understand that excess inventory is not caused solely by the desire to maintain a 99 percent or higher customer service level. Another contributor to excess inventory is the desire to carry safety stock as a cushion against demand forecast inaccuracy. Most enterprise resource planning and advance planning and scheduling systems have functions that calculate a recommended safety stock level. These calculations are partially based on demand forecast accuracy. The lower the accuracy, the greater the safety stock calculation. We often cover our forecasting sins with excess inventory.

Case in point: I recently worked with a consumer goods manufacturer that struggled with forecast accuracy on a particular product. Forecast accuracy averaged 70 percent one week out in the future at the corporate planning level. This product should not have been that difficult to forecast. It was a high-volume, basic replenishment consumable that was rarely promoted.

In trying to determine how to forecast with a higher degree of reliability, we found that the retailer customer communicated a demand forecast that was 92 percent accurate at the distribution center level thirty days out in the future. The retailer's demand forecast was largely ignored by the manufacturer, however.

In investigating why the retailer's demand forecast was not considered, we found that a formal means of collaboration had not been established between the companies. This caused a lack of trust in the retailer's forecast numbers by the manufacturer. This lack of trust was costly to the consumer goods manufacturer as well as the retailer. Until the demand plan accuracy improved, the bullwhip effect could not be reduced. Unless the bullwhip could be reduced, it would be difficult for both partners to increase sales revenue, reduce inventory, and increase profit margins.

After all, if you think about it, there is only one reason for companies to be in business. That is to make a profit. Profits generate cash that can be put to all sorts of uses, such as investing in new products, processes, systems, and people and rewarding employees, management, and shareholders alike. Wal-Mart has always recognized the value and need to create profit. It was one reason that spurred the company to pioneer supply chain collaboration. In the next chapter, Wal-Mart's success in supply chain collaboration is reviewed.

SUMMARY OF BEST PRACTICES IN MINIMIZING THE BULLWHIP EFFECT

1. All enterprises in the supply chain have visibility of consumer demand history and they strive to be consumer centric rather than just customer centric.
2. The business closest to the point of consumption communicates a forecast of demand and other pertinent demand information to its trading partners.
3. It is recognized that accurate demand information is the key to reducing the bullwhip effect.
4. The financial impact of the bullwhip effect is understood by trading partners.
5. Trading partners work cooperatively to minimize the bullwhip effect. This is a continuous effort.
6. The financial consequences of reactive processes are recognized and trading partners are working to develop responsive processes in their place.
7. Impediments to gaining a greater visibility of demand are recognized and actions are taken to remove those impediments.
8. Trading partner information is utilized in each trading partner's planning processes.
9. Employees who interact with customers, including salespeople and customer facing teams, serve as conduits for communicating customer information within their companies. They are not information gatekeepers.
10. It is recognized that trading partner information will not always be 100 percent correct. The collaboration process includes methods for communicating questions about the trading partner information and for identifying and correcting errors.
11. A formal means of collaboration is developed between trading partners. The formalization of the relationship addresses trust and other cultural issues that could prevent the companies from working together to reduce the bullwhip effect.

QUESTIONS

1. What happens when there is a bullwhip effect in the supply chain?
2. Why does the bullwhip effect occur?
3. What is the financial impact of the bullwhip effect?
4. What role does visibility of point-of-consumption demand play in reducing the bullwhip effect?
5. Why are reactive processes less advantageous than responsive processes?

6. What is the difference between consumer centric and customer centric?
7. What is the risk in taking demand information communicated by customers at face value?
8. In the case examples that were presented, what were the consequences of lack of trust?

3

WAL-MART CASE EXAMPLE

Adversarial. That is the best way to characterize Wal-Mart and Procter & Gamble's relationship in the late 1980s. Every time founder Sam Walton and Wal-Mart executives met with Procter & Gamble's executives, it was like the meeting of two gorillas, both trying to position themselves as the dominant partner to control the ultimate decision.

The relationship deteriorated to the point that Walton and executives from Procter & Gamble decided to intervene. They scheduled a meeting with executives from both companies. The purpose of the meeting was for the companies to determine how to forge a new relationship based on leveraging their individual strengths.

Robert Bruce, former Vice President of Wal-Mart's Inventory Management and Supply Chain, characterizes the meeting as a turning point for both companies. As it turned out, it was a turning point for the retail industry as well. This meeting was the start of supply chain collaboration as we know it today and was the genesis of a new business model for the retail industry.

Bruce remembers how Walton finally convinced both parties to stop feuding and start cooperating. Walton observed that Wal-Mart was in the business of merchandising and selling products to the end consumer, and Procter & Gamble was in the business of manufacturing and shipping the right products to sell to Wal-Mart. Walton told the group, "Why don't we just work together and get the job done in the most efficient way possible? It's simple. You ship us product and we'll send you money."

While the actual execution is more complicated than that, it was hard to argue with Walton's logic. And to those attending the meeting, it was perfectly obvious how both companies handicapped themselves by treating each other like an enemy.

From this meeting, a new business relationship evolved. Instead of focusing on dominance over one another, they shifted to how the companies could bring their respective *competencies* to dominate the *marketplace.*

In the case of Wal-Mart and all retailers, a core competency needs to be in merchandising. This involves making sure that the products consumers want to buy are on the store shelves and competitively priced. For Procter & Gamble and companies that supply products to retailers, a core competency needs to be in producing quality products that the consumers want or need, shipping the products in the proper quantities to retailers at the right time, and providing marketing to stimulate consumers to buy the products. If the retailer and supplier (or both) are less than competent, both parties (and the supplier's suppliers) suffer. Products are not available to sell, and if they are available, getting them on the store shelves requires actions that erode profit margins. This is why some industry experts and practitioners are beginning to view the supply chain as a *profit* chain.

Walton believed that if Wal-Mart and Procter & Gamble worked together instead of against each other, they could leverage their core competencies so that both companies would be more financially successful. Figuring out how to break down barriers between Wal-Mart and its suppliers had been on Sam Walton's mind for quite some time. In his autobiography, Walton explained his thinking:

> Communicate everything you possibly can to your partners. The more they know, the more they'll understand. The more they understand, the more they'll care. Once they care, there's no stopping them.*

Sam Walton was a long-time supporter of using technology as a business investment as well as a competitive advantage. It was during the mid to late 1980s that Wal-Mart started to put pieces in place for communicating information to suppliers. Under Walton's direction, Wal-Mart began developing the technology capability to share retail information with its trading partners, such as point-of-sale data, inventory levels, and point-of-sale forecasts.

It became clear, however, that more than technology capability was needed to break down barriers between Wal-Mart and its suppliers. Even within Wal-Mart, the attitude and behaviors toward its suppliers did not encourage partnering,

---

* Walton, Sam and Huey, John, *Made in America: My Story,* Doubleday, 1992, p. 247.

collaborating, and working together to better serve customers and the market-place. That was one reason Walton helped broker the meeting with Procter & Gamble's executives.

Wal-Mart's tremendous success in the 1990s and into the 2000s was influenced by four factors that separate Wal-Mart and other highly successful companies from mediocre firms. First, Wal-Mart dared to challenge the current business rules and to articulate a new business model. Second, Wal-Mart found creative ways to address the cultural issues that prevented its suppliers and its own associates from adopting the new business model. Third, Wal-Mart understood that technology would be necessary to enable conveying consumer and other retail information to its suppliers. Fourth, Wal-Mart was impatient and refused to wait for the planets to be aligned properly (meaning technology, trading partners, and its own associates) to implement supply chain collaboration.

Unlike most retailers in the 1980s and early 1990s, Wal-Mart was willing to invest in information technology to support its supply chain collaboration vision. Wal-Mart's earliest efforts at communicating point-of-sale data and replenishment schedules to trading partners involved using electronic data interchange (EDI) as the information conduit. As technology advanced, Wal-Mart developed a private exchange, called Retail Link, to provide trading partners with ready access to Wal-Mart information.

In developing technology to support supply chain collaboration, Wal-Mart overturned a long-standing practice in the retail industry. Wal-Mart provided its retail information for *free*, which was counter to the norm in the retail industry in the 1980s. In fact, it was considered revolutionary by industry insiders and blasphemous by others. At several industry conferences in the mid-1990s, CEOs and other executives of retail companies vowed never to share point-of-sale data with their suppliers.

Wal-Mart was not bashful about redefining business rules. The company's actions are in concert with what Gary Hamel and C.K. Prahalad observe in their book, *Competing for the Future,* that it takes to be an industry leader:

> To create a future, a company must change in some fundamental way the rules of engagement in a long-standing industry.*

Walton recognized that the business rules needed to change if Wal-Mart was to dominate its competitors and achieve greater profit margins in a profit-stingy

---

* Hamel, Gary and Prahalad, C.K., *Competing for the Future,* Harvard Business School Press, 1994, p. 21.

industry. By providing data to its trading partners free of charge, Wal-Mart challenged more than just an industry-accepted business practice. More significantly, Wal-Mart challenged the prevailing mind-set about the relationship between retailers and their suppliers that fostered mistrust and adversarial behavior toward one another.

Prior to Wal-Mart's redefining the rules on sharing data, retailers and third parties, like Kmart, sold point-of-sale information to their suppliers. Selling point-of-sale data was considered simply a business transaction and a revenue stream. Suppliers primarily used this information as market intelligence that aided decisions about marketing programs and promotions. Point-of-sale information prior to the late 1980s was rarely communicated to the supply side of the organizations for informed decisions about demand planning and supply planning.

With the exception of Sam Walton and Wal-Mart, few retailers thought about the value of providing retailer and consumer information to suppliers to assist in supply chain planning. The orientation of most companies in the industry then was on merchandising and marketing. There was much less interest in ensuring that the right amount of stock was on the shelves without requiring unnecessary investment in safety stock. Leaders of companies had little awareness of the value of an effective supply chain. In fact, supply chain management was not even in most executives' vocabularies at the time.

Wal-Mart perceived correctly that if its trading partners had better visibility of point-of-sale consumption and future consumer demand, both Wal-Mart and its trading partners could reduce inventory and other wasted activities throughout the supply chain. By doing so, costs could be removed from the supply chain and the savings could be passed along to consumers. Consumers would be more satisfied with both the price and the fact that product they wanted to buy was on the shelf. The result would be increased consumer loyalty, which in turn would increase sales. This was the supply chain strategy that Wal-Mart envisioned as its future competitive advantage.

The rub in this strategy was extending the business enterprise beyond Wal-Mart's own walls to encompass the supply chain. This idea of an extended enterprise was novel in the 1980s and met resistance (and still does) by Wal-Mart's trading partners. To overcome resistance, Wal-Mart worked diligently (even today, more than a decade later) to convince its trading partners to adopt supply chain collaboration in a meaningful way.

In 2002, Randy Salley, a Vice President of Information Technology at Wal-Mart, spoke at a conference on the merits of the UCCNet. He explained the savings that suppliers and Wal-Mart could realize if they all agreed to utilize this technology to synchronize data. A supplier representative remarked that his own corporate management resisted joining the UCCNet and he wished that

Wal-Mart would just make it mandatory. Salley replied, "We could make it mandatory, but that sure doesn't sound very collaborative."*

Why does Wal-Mart keep pushing the supply chain collaboration business model? The answer goes to the heart of Wal-Mart's philosophy. Pleasing the consumer has always been Wal-Mart's primary philosophy. Unlike many companies that have come to dominate markets and then raise their prices, Wal-Mart passes its cost savings along to consumers as part of its effort to continually please its customers. Wal-Mart strives to dominate the market through customer loyalty and understands that if it does not take care of the consumer, then a competitor will.

As early as the mid-1980s, Sam Walton and Wal-Mart executives understood that supply chain collaboration would enable the company to be more consumer centric than in the past. It would also enable Wal-Mart to be more responsive to individual store demographics than in the past. This would enable Wal-Mart to develop a highly targeted and customized approach to consumers, rather than using a more generic regional- or distribution-center-based marketing approach.

The practicality of using supply chain collaboration to become more consumer centric evolved over time, starting with just-in-time techniques and advancing with vendor managed inventory and efficient consumer response programs. Figure 7 documents the evolution of various approaches utilized by Wal-Mart and the retail industry that have led to supply chain collaboration.

Each step of these preliminary steps toward supply chain collaboration was successful in stripping inventory from the supply chain and improving companies' ability to ensure product availability. Each of these steps had limitations, however. Chief among the limitations was the lack of visibility of consumer sales history and retailer demand plans and replenishment needs. Thus, the supplier continued to be forced to guess or estimate the retailers' demand, which kept the bullwhip effect alive and well in the supply chain.

Wal-Mart saw the virtue of shifting to a demand-driven supply chain enterprise and began communicating consumer demand information to its trading partners many years prior to other retailers. Using a demand-driven approach is often called a pull-based strategy. With this approach, consumer purchases trigger replenishment by suppliers, which in turn triggers replenishment of the suppliers' material and components, and so on throughout the supply chain. For a demand-driven, pull-based strategy to work most effectively, all links in the value chain must have access to a single demand plan or forecast. This single demand plan is based on consumer consumption and retailer replenishment schedules and is communicated throughout the extended enterprise.

---

* Retail Systems Conference, Chicago's McCormick Center, June 2002.

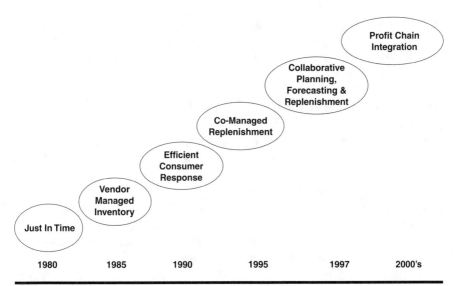

Figure 7. Evolution of Supply Chain Collaboration. (Reprinted with permission from VCC Associates, Inc.)

The challenge for Wal-Mart was getting its own planning managers and buyers, as well as its trading partners, to focus on replenishing product at the stores, rather than at the distribution centers. The business model prior to the demand-driven, pull-based strategy was to replenish product at the distribution center and then expect the distribution center to push product through the supply chain to the stores (oftentimes, whether or not the stores needed the product). This is known as a push strategy.

While working at Wal-Mart, I recall frequently being reminded by Wal-Mart's executives that if we were not working on helping the stores, we were working on the wrong thing. It was a well-known fact that Walton and his strong team of corporate executives believed that the most important people in the company were (and are) the store associates.

The information technology group at Wal-Mart was not exempt from this philosophy. Having gained my information technology experience in the aerospace and defense industry, I had to adjust my mind-set to Wal-Mart's philosophy. Wal-Mart's programmers are taught to be retailers first and programmers second. Several times during each year, I found myself and my programmers sent to work with the users of our technology at stores and distribution centers. Many of us were also expected to work as associates in the stores and distribution centers for at least one week each year. I also found myself traveling with Wal-Mart executives to the stores and distribution centers at least two to three weeks per month. The ultimate goal of the information technology organization was to develop the technology solutions that the end user actually needed by having the information technology group know and understand how the business actually worked.

Needless to say, this experience was an eye opener. There is an old saying in the world of computer programming: "We developed exactly what the user asked for, not necessarily what they needed." Wal-Mart's approach forced the information technology group to become savvy about what the associates really wanted and needed to support the stores and, ultimately, the consumers. This savvy became very useful as Wal-Mart began to develop supply chain collaboration processes. It also enabled Wal-Mart to push ahead in its effort.

Wal-Mart was impatient to implement consumer-driven supply chain collaboration and replenishment with its trading partners. The company chose not to wait for technology firms to develop the software to support supply chain collaboration. It would have taken too long. Wal-Mart's information technology group developed pull-based, automated store-level replenishment systems, point-of-sale systems, a perpetual inventory system, software for handheld radio frequency devices, micromerchandising applications, as well as a host of other technology — all in support of the store.

The experiences in developing these software applications, as well as our experience in working with users of the technology at the stores and distribution centers, prepared us to develop store-level forecasting applications. This was no small feat when you consider the scale of a company like Wal-Mart. Think about the number of Wal-Mart stores and the number of products carried in each store. It amounts to generating replenishment forecasts for more than two hundred million store items over a fifty-two-week rolling horizon.

The important point to remember about these forecasts: They are tied directly to the automated replenishment systems for the stores and distribution centers, which communicate replenishment needs and schedules to Wal-Mart's trading partners. If the demand forecasts are wrong, so is the replenishment plan and schedule, which creates the bullwhip effect throughout the supply chain. Forecast, or demand plan, accuracy becomes paramount to realizing the benefits of collaboration for all trading partners.

The need for accurate demand forecasts led Wal-Mart to the next step, co-managed replenishment, in its evolution toward value chain collaboration. In the early 1990s, Robert Bruce recognized that a team of Wal-Mart forecast analysts was needed to share forecasts with suppliers and collaborate with them to improve forecast accuracy. Bruce understood that improving forecast accuracy requires more than technology; it requires communication among partners and judgment. If discipline was used to document the collaborative judgments, the replenishment order policy file rules in the software system could be updated and made more accurate.

By focusing on how to improve forecast accuracy, Bruce quickly perceived a significant impediment — the forecasting process was too departmentalized. Buyers, replenishment analysts, warehousing, transportation, and store operations based replenishment plans on their own individual demand forecasts. These individual forecasts did not tie directly to the centralized replenishment system. The replenishment system was based on point-of-sale data, which made it more customer driven than the other individual forecasts.

The end result was multiple, disparate views of demand that were not reconciled into a single forecast that all departments used to base their plans. Because these different views were technology based with little judgment applied to them, one might call this situation "islands of automation." The end effect was to create a bullwhip effect.

Bruce believed a single demand forecast, derived through collaboration, should ultimately drive the replenishment systems and operational plans across the entire supply chain. This meant that Wal-Mart's suppliers would also base their replenishment and operational plans on the Wal-Mart forecast and would collaborate to develop this single forecast.

There were some challenges to this approach. First was the sheer volume of data. With millions of end items to plan, technology was needed to communicate a single forecast throughout Wal-Mart's internal supply chain as well as to its supplier base. Wal-Mart's information technology group developed vendor forecasting technology that enabled transmitting information via EDI and Retail Link. This information included point-of-sale demand forecasts at the store level that could be aggregated up to the distribution center level as well as the five thousand suppliers at corporate level.

As it turned out, communicating point-of-sale forecasts to the supplier community did not mean that the suppliers would use the forecasts to drive their replenishment and operational plans. Here were the hitches from the suppliers' point of view: They challenged the accuracy of the forecasts and the forecasts did not represent a commitment by Wal-Mart to purchase the volume and timing of product represented in the forecasts.

Ironically, Wal-Mart did not expect suppliers to take the forecasts at face value. Wal-Mart understood that the forecasts would be inaccurate, and that is why the company wanted to collaborate with its trading partners. Wal-Mart expected suppliers to add their market knowledge to the forecast and work with Wal-Mart's buyers and planners to refine and adjust the forecasts. Suppliers would provide information on causal factors, such as a product's seasonality at the distribution center and store levels, consumer preferences in different geographic locations, planned promotions and the resulting increase in demand, and new item introductions, to name a few factors. This would provide greater insight on the timing and volume fluctuations of demand, which in turn would improve forecast accuracy.

Today, the collaborative approach between Wal-Mart and its suppliers remains uneven. Many suppliers simply do not use Wal-Mart's demand forecasts to drive their own replenishment and planning processes. Nor do they collaborate by providing their own demand-related information. As a result, a bullwhip effect remains in the Wal-Mart supply chain.

The desire for firm orders to drive production plans and inventory plans is another reason why suppliers have been reluctant partners with Wal-Mart. Procter & Gamble diminished this problem by using distribution resource planning logic and technology to convert Wal-Mart's point-of-sale forecast and point-of-sale history into order-point calculations. The calculations are based on the ordering rules of lead times, pack sizes, and target shelf quantities.

While the partner arrangement falls short of Wal-Mart communicating firm orders, the information on inventory at the store levels, demand forecasts, and point-of-sale history still have value to suppliers. When this information is added to suppliers' own future promotion and new item introduction plans, more accurate demand forecasts are created.

Still, this approach does not address suppliers' concern about risk. Without a commitment to purchase over some near-term time frame, the supplier assumes more risk for the consequence of forecast errors. For key suppliers, like Procter & Gamble, which did not choose to ignore the information provided by Wal-Mart, forecast accuracy improved, resulting in a dampening of the bullwhip effect. This resulted in lowering risk and resulted in reduced inventory and increased sales.

As Wal-Mart and its suppliers began to collaborate, the question was not whether demand collaboration was worthwhile. Instead, the focus shifted to the amount of labor required to collaborate and adjust demand forecasts on the corporate level, let alone the store level. It was just too labor intensive to be practical.

Even Procter & Gamble, a company known for foresight and willingness to pioneer supply chain management techniques, found it too labor intensive to collaborate beyond the distribution center. Given the amount of labor and time required to collaborate on demand forecasts at the store level, Procter & Gamble preferred to continue using vendor managed inventory to supply the distribution centers and ignore the store-level demands on the distribution centers.

The practical limitations of performing demand collaboration at the store level was the impetus for providing automation in support of co-managed replenishment. A meeting with a hosiery supplier spurred Wal-Mart to address this prickly issue.

During the meeting, the supplier complained that the agreed forecast adjustments were not making it into the replenishment system, which wasted its and Wal-Mart's effort in collaborating. Wal-Mart associates told the supplier that there simply was not enough time to make all of the agreed adjustments.

In listening to the experience recounted by the supplier, Robert Bruce, Bob Blankenship (the director of the distribution center replenishment at the time), and I asked ourselves: Why not train suppliers how to use Wal-Mart's replenishment and forecasting technology tools? Why not give suppliers remote access to these tools through the Internet? That way, they could make the forecast adjustments themselves at the appropriate levels. This would compress the time required to calculate, communicate, and then input the adjustments in the system. This approach would provide a single technology platform and planning methodology for Wal-Mart and its suppliers to communicate, review, and adjust demand forecasts and replenishment plans.

A widely noted shortcoming of vendor managed inventory and forecast collaboration had been that trading partners used different planning methods and technology. This limitation could be overcome by giving suppliers access to Wal-Mart's replenishment and forecasting tools. Robert Bruce termed this approach co-managed replenishment because it promoted jointly managing demand to refine replenishment plans and improve forecast accuracy. It also would bring Wal-Mart closer to achieving a long-desired aim — developing a consumer-driven demand plan that could be communicated throughout the supply chain.

Within one year, Wal-Mart quickly piloted the co-managed replenishment process with four strategic suppliers. The results were outstanding. Forecast accuracies at the store shelf improved an average of 10 percent for basic merchandise and forecast accuracy on promoted items improved as much as 40 percent. This resulted in reduced out-of-stock items at the store level, increased sales revenue, and made it possible to reduce safety stock.

It is important to point out that technology alone did not make the pilots successful. The key to success was the competence of the people within Wal-Mart and the strategic suppliers that promoted communication between the partners.

The co-managed replenishment pilot programs broke new ground for forming closer partner relationships. The strategic suppliers were given offices inside Wal-Mart's general offices that were located near Wal-Mart's buyers and inventory managers. With ready access to one another, openness and trust developed and problem solving became more collaborative, cooperative, and routine.

Spurred by the successful pilots, Wal-Mart aggressively rolled out co-managed replenishment to its key suppliers. Eventually more than three hundred key suppliers engaged in the program. Wal-Mart provided the suppliers with training on the process and technology. Once the training was complete, the key suppliers were given remote access and update authority in Wal-Mart's replenishment system via the Internet, using Wal-Mart's private exchange, Retail Link.

At this point, it would be nice to report that everyone lived happily ever after, but this is not the end of the story. Many suppliers did not embrace co-managed replenishment. Some suppliers resisted changing their internal processes and methodology. Other suppliers lacked corporate support, people skills, and technology capability to participate in co-managed replenishment.

Among those suppliers that resisted change, some made the conscious choice not to engage in these types of programs until it was mandated by their retailer customers. We call these companies "Old World Suppliers." They want to keep doing what they have always done and lack the ability to envision transformational strategies that will improve their companies' financial performance. The losers are not just the resistant suppliers, but their suppliers as well.

Old World Suppliers still exist today. You see them at conferences where many of them serve as members of committees. In an exquisite dance of passive resistance, they are more than willing to study the new processes, but never implement them.

The lack of engagement by many of Wal-Mart's supplier community drove Wal-Mart's executives to another conclusion. Wal-Mart could not go it alone. Other retailers must also implement co-managed replenishment so that it would become not a best practice, but a standard industry practice.

The majority of retailers and suppliers would have to embrace co-managed replenishment to prevent Wal-Mart's efforts from being marginalized. In 1995, Wal-Mart represented less than 15 percent of sales revenues for many of its suppliers. For co-managed replenishment to be a worthwhile investment for Wal-Mart's suppliers, we calculated that 50 to 60 percent of the suppliers' key retailer customers needed to adopt similar collaborative programs. This rate of adoption would enable suppliers to reduce their bullwhip effect with their suppliers and transportation firms. The resulting optimization of the supply chain processes would yield the financial benefits needed to make the effort of financial value to suppliers.

For the collaboration processes that Wal-Mart had pioneered to become standard in the industry, suppliers needed the ability to readily manage multiple retailers' demand forecasts. That was the subject of a meeting that Randy Mott, Wal-Mart's CIO at the time, asked me to attend in Cambridge, Massachusetts with a small industry analyst firm, Benchmarking Partners. The purpose of the meeting was to discuss how to create a pilot program to model an industry standard for co-managed replenishment. We named the pilot program Collaborative Forecasting and Replenishment (CFAR).

The discussions at the meeting were enlightening. We knew that an industry standard would not be successful unless it provided financial benefits for all trading partners. We also knew from Wal-Mart's co-managed replenishment effort that technology did not guarantee success. People and their approach to business were the drivers for success.

Retailers and suppliers alike had to be willing to break widely accepted business paradigms. For example, Wal-Mart's and other retailers' buyers needed to be trained not to cancel an order at the last minute so as not to create a supply chain bullwhip effect in responding to the change. On the flip side, suppliers needed to be trained not to offer retailers last-minute price discounts and other deals to meet monthly or quarterly sales quotas.

To illustrate the effect of such behavior, performance metrics needed to be identified that quantified the impact of business practices that reduced and increased the bullwhip effect in the supply chain.

The discussions during the meeting with Benchmarking Partners drove us to the realization that it was relatively easy to define the best technology to support supply chain collaboration. It was going to be harder and take more time to develop the awareness and understanding of why old business paradigms needed to change. So we made the conscious decision to focus first on developing the case for change and defining the collaborative processes, and then we would identify industry standard technology enablers.

As a starting point, the CFAR team defined how information and decisions should ideally flow in a collaborative forecasting and replenishment process through the development of what we called "use cases." These use cases also enabled us to begin to define the technology needed to support the process.

After completing the use cases, we quickly piloted the concept to determine additional refinements that were needed. Warner-Lambert and its Listerine® product line were selected for the twelve-week pilot with Wal-Mart. Using just one product line would keep the pilot simple.

We also wanted to keep the technology relatively simple, so we leveraged Wal-Mart's replenishment analyst, Julie Heckschler, informally known as Computer Julie, and Warner-Lambert's, Bob Uccardi, informally known as Computer Bob, to act as the collaboration software. In short, the collaborative pilot was done manually, with Computer Bob onsite at the Wal-Mart corporate headquarters, located next to Computer Julie. The only technology that was used was the current store and distribution center automated replenishment applications and the point-of-sales forecasts that were created by the replenish-

Basic Side Counter Forecast Accuracy
- Store level: From 80 to 92 percent
- Distribution center: Remained at 95 percent

Promoted Items Forecast Accuracy
- Store level: From 50 to 82 percent
- Distribution center: From 50 to 88 percent

Inventory and In-Stock Results
- In-stock in stores: From 87 to 98 percent
- On-hand inventory: Reduced by two weeks of supply

Lead Time Results
- Lead time: From twenty-one to eleven days

Sales Revenue Results
- Increased sales revenue by $8.5 million

Figure 8. Warner-Lambert Listerine® Pilot Results.

ment engine. The actual collaboration between the two trading partners was manual.

With the help of Heckschler and Uccardi, we leveraged technology resources from Wal-Mart, Warner-Lambert, Benchmarking Partners, SAP, and Manugistics to document how the process needed to flow differently to be more effective and scalable. We also identified performance metrics that would give a balanced view for both the supplier and retailer on the effectiveness of the process and the financial results. From this effort, scorecards were drafted and financial incentives for partnering were identified. Finally, Heckschler and Uccardi provided input from a process user point of view on the technology requirements for supporting collaborative planning and replenishment.

It is interesting to note that even with a simple approach to the twelve-week pilot, the collaborative effort yielded significant results for Wal-Mart and Warner-Lambert (see Figure 8). Warner-Lambert was also named Wal-Mart's vendor of the year.

Viewing these results, it was not difficult to extrapolate the benefits that could be achieved if at least 50 percent of the companies operating in the consumer goods industry joined the effort. The next step was to create awareness throughout the industry of the financial benefit from supply chain collaboration. This meant reaching out to suppliers and retailers alike.

We documented the results from the Warner-Lambert Listerine® pilot as well as Wal-Mart's earlier experiences in collaborating with strategic and key suppliers. More than two hundred retailers and consumer goods manufacturers were invited to attend a presentation at Harvard Business School where we outlined the collaboration concept and process structure and showed the pilot results. We also made a similar presentation at a meeting for the grocery industry.

The companies participating in these meetings expressed interest in developing an industry standard for supply chain collaboration. It was decided that the Voluntary Interindustry Commerce Standards (VICS) committee provided the proper forum for defining an industry standard, and a subcommittee was formed. Wal-Mart's Robert Bruce was joined by Joe Andraski, then the Vice President of Customer Marketing at Nabisco, and Ralph Drayer, Vice President of Customer Service at Procter & Gamble. In early discussions among subcommittee members, it was pointed out that the planning component of collaboration was missing from the CFAR title. Thus, the term Collaborative Planning, Forecasting, and Replenishment (CPFR®) was born. (The evolution of CPFR® processes and practices will be addressed further later in this book.)

More than ten years after the Wal-Mart and Procter & Gamble meeting, their desire to work together more collaboratively has spawned a new business model, new business processes and practices, and new technology to support trading information among supply chain partners. For Wal-Mart, supply chain collaboration has been part of a transformational strategy that has enabled it to eliminate waste from its supply chain and pass along the savings to its customers. Wal-Mart has been rewarded for its effort with sales revenues that have risen nearly 15 percent per year. (See Figures 9 and 10 for other Wal-Mart financial performance measures.)

While some competitors, suppliers, and others in corporate America fear that Wal-Mart has become too powerful, a Cannondale Associates survey of 122 manufacturers revealed that Wal-Mart was the "best retailer with which to do business."* Why? In changing the rules of doing business with Wal-Mart, Wal-Mart has eliminated various fees, such as slotting and display fees, and other extraneous costs that were passed on to Wal-Mart and its customers. This approach strips away distractions from focusing on what consumers want to buy. Wal-Mart's Every Day Low Pricing policy also has resulted in more predictable volumes of product, which gives the company's suppliers the opportunity to reduce their bullwhip effect and improve their profit margins.

Changing the business rules has also provided opportunity for Wal-Mart's suppliers to improve their companies' financial performance. For Procter & Gamble, the new way of doing business has bolstered its footing in the extremely competitive consumer goods industry. Procter & Gamble has also used

---

* Useem, Jerry, One nation under Wal-Mart: how retailing's superpower — and our biggest most admired company — is changing the rules for corporate America, *Fortune,* February 18, 2003.

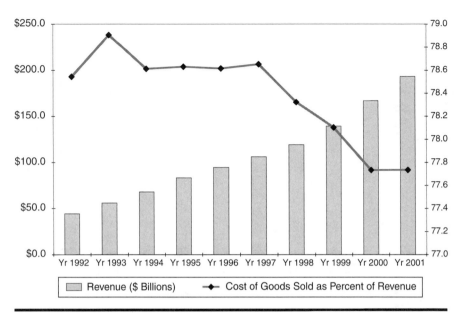

Figure 9.   Wal-Mart Financial Performance.

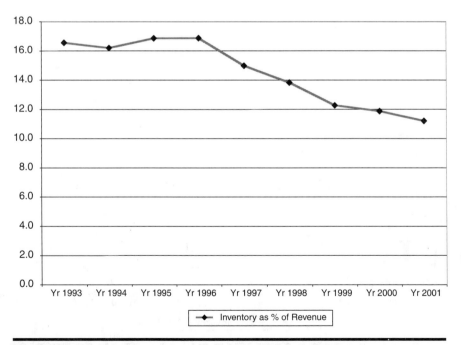

Figure 10.   Wal-Mart Inventory as a Percent of Revenue.

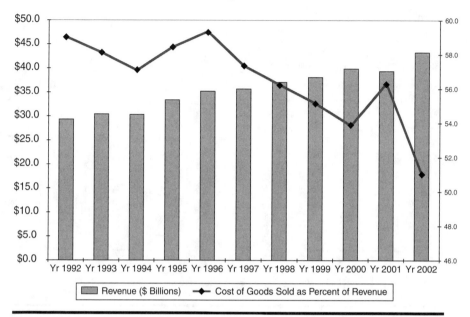

Figure 11.   Procter & Gamble Financial Performance.

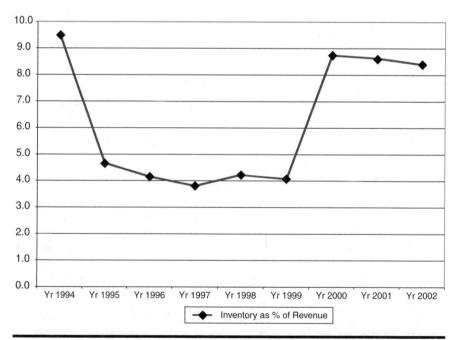

Figure 12.   Procter & Gamble Inventory as a Percent of Revenue.

its leverage in the marketplace to convince its other retailer customers to adopt supply chain collaboration. As a result, Procter & Gamble continues to thrive as evidenced by its financial performance (Figures 11 and 12).

From adversaries to partners, Wal-Mart and Procter & Gamble have proved to the industry that when companies work together toward a common vision, both companies win.

QUESTIONS

1. Why was Wal-Mart and Procter & Gamble having an adversarial relationship in the 1980s?
2. What was the importance of technology for Wal-Mart?
3. What four factors did Wal-Mart use in the 1990s and 2000s to separate itself from its competition?
4. What is co-managed replenishment?
5. What was CFAR?
6. Why did Wal-Mart believe that supply chain collaboration needed to be an industry standard?

WARNER-LAMBERT CASE EXAMPLE

In the previous chapter, we highlighted the success of Warner-Lambert and Wal-Mart's pilot of CFAR, but there is much more to the Warner-Lambert story. It is both a cautionary tale and a success story.

Let's recount the Warner-Lambert experience through Jay Nearnberg's viewpoint. In the spring of 1995, he was the Director of Customer Replenishment for Warner-Lambert. In this capacity, Nearnberg was not looking forward to an upcoming meeting with Wal-Mart's buyer.

Warner-Lambert, before being acquired by Pfizer in 2001, produced household health and beauty care products as well as pharmaceuticals. Its Listerine® product was, and still is, a top seller. At that time, Listerine® could sell much more than its current performance, but product availability problems kept the product from getting on store shelves. Out-of-stock situations with Wal-Mart and other retail customers were the norm.

Nearnberg knew that the inability to keep product on store shelves and in the distribution centers was costing Warner-Lambert millions of dollars in lost sales as well as credibility with its retail customers and consumers. To Nearnberg's credit, his approach to the upcoming Wal-Mart meeting was not to be defensive or to try to placate the buyer. Rather, he admitted there was a problem and asked for help. He wanted to leverage Wal-Mart's supply chain experience and insight to help structure improvements at Warner-Lambert.

Nearnberg was astute in understanding that there was more than one reason for the product availability problems. Obviously, Warner-Lambert's internal planning processes were ineffective. He also believed that the way Warner-Lambert interacted with its retail customers in planning demand and replenishment was a key part of the problem.

The time was ripe to spearhead change within Warner-Lambert to address the product availability issues. The company's senior executive team was aware of Wal-Mart's edict: Improve in-stock levels to 98 percent or else we will cut back the shelf space for your basic merchandise, stop buying promotions, and will not add new products. This ultimatum was the subject of a presentation, entitled "Ninety-eight Percent or Else," that Nearnberg, with the help of his team, made to corporate executives and management functions that contributed to service performance levels.

So it was with a sense of urgency that Nearnberg reached out to his various contacts at Wal-Mart following his meeting with the buyer. He visited with Charlie McMurtry, the Director of Wal-Mart's Retail Link group, to discuss Wal-Mart's approach to demand forecasting. Charlie told Jay that Warner-Lambert could access point-of-sale history and a sixty-five-week forecast through Wal-Mart's Retail Link. Jay inquired about Wal-Mart's automated replenishment system that was outlined in Chapter 3.

Like most of Wal-Mart's suppliers at the time, Jay was aware that Warner-Lambert did not make use of the information and tools offered suppliers by Wal-Mart. Why not? It was well known that Wal-Mart's demand forecasts and replenishment schedules were inaccurate. There also would be challenges in integrating a single customer's forecasts into production planning without additional customers' critical mass also included.

As Jay and I discussed the intent of Wal-Mart's collaboration effort, I emphasized that Wal-Mart assumed that its trading partners would provide feedback; in other words, collaborate to improve the accuracy of the forecast and replenishment schedules. The replenishment plan was based on the forecast, so it was imperative to create as accurate a demand forecast as possible. The more accurate the forecast, the more accurate the replenishment schedule would be.

The structure and intent of Wal-Mart's approach to collaboration made sense to Jay, and he set about a fact-finding mission that involved Warner-Lambert and Wal-Mart planners. Warehouse withdrawals in the distribution centers were evaluated to help determine why Wal-Mart's distribution centers kept running out of Warner-Lambert products.

Warner-Lambert's Marie Taylor and Bob Uccardi analyzed the withdrawal transactions and found that Wal-Mart's distribution centers' forecasts were not synchronized with the store-level forecasts. In other words, planning was being done in silos rather than for the entire supply chain. The analysis also showed that Wal-Mart's forecasts did not take into account the correct seasonality of demand or planned promotions. Further analysis showed shelf space may have been too low in some stores to support consumer demand.

As Warner-Lambert's team worked with Wal-Mart's planners, they were able to demonstrate that consumer demand (point-of-sale demand) for Warner-Lambert products was actually fairly predictable, especially when the products were not being promoted. Listerine®, for example, had an extremely predictable and consistent weekly consumer demand.

The analysis of the findings reinforced for Wal-Mart that it was imperative for its trading partners to review and provide feedback on the forecasts. Without this review and collaboration, the inaccuracies in the forecast had impact up and down the supply chain and ultimately created consumer dissatisfaction when the product consumers wanted to buy was not on the store shelf.

With these findings in mind, Nearnberg met with Robert Bruce, Vice President of Wal-Mart's Inventory Management and Forecasting group. Bruce oversaw a team of forecast analysts led by the Director of Forecasting, Mike Casey. Nearnberg wanted to learn how Wal-Mart created demand forecasts and how a trading partner could link into the process by providing information on seasonality indexes, historical promotional lifts, and planned promotions.

Nearnberg believed that demand collaboration could help solve Warner-Lambert's service difficulties with Wal-Mart. He envisioned Warner-Lambert's analysts regularly collaborating with Wal-Mart's forecast analysts to develop more accurate profiles of seasonality indexes and promotional lifts. Wal-Mart's analysts could then apply these adjustments to the forecast algorithms. The end result would be a much improved forecast of demand, which then would create more accurate replenishment schedules and orders. If this process could be done well and with regularity, store in-stock levels would improve and safety stock levels could be reduced.

In performing the analysis and discussing ways to collaborate, examples of the need for collaboration emerged. One dramatic example was a July 4th high-value coupon in a roto circular for a Schick Women's Razor. The Wal-Mart team knew that a coupon would be distributed in Sunday newspapers nationwide, but did not believe the coupons would significantly impact demand. Warner-Lambert's analysts knew from past experience that the coupons would create a sizable lift in demand and suggested increasing the demand forecast by 5 percent. Wal-Mart analysts countered with a 3 percent lift. The actual increase in demand was 9 percent. Rather than criticize each other over the missed sales opportunity, both parties agreed to learn from the experience and include the newfound promotion lift knowledge in the forecast the next time the product was promoted.

As Warner-Lambert and Wal-Mart worked together during the next three months to better collaborate on demand forecasts, the value of collaborating became readily apparent. In one case, Warner-Lambert began to provide demand seasonality information for cough and cold medicines. The seasonality indexes had been developed as a result of extensive research by Warner-Lambert. Prior to this time, Warner-Lambert had not shared this information with Wal-Mart. It became obvious to Wal-Mart that Warner-Lambert was a reliable source of information on promotional lifts and the ramp-up cycles of new item introductions. There just were not enough hours in the day for Wal-Mart's analysts to develop this information on every one of its suppliers' products. Wal-Mart has over five thousand suppliers.

This experience reinforced the need to blend the best retail knowledge of information with the supplier's knowledge of information. By doing so, the customer and the supplier could generate far more accurate forecasts than either party alone could develop. This was needed to smooth the supply chain bullwhip that was causing both companies to lose sales.

In just three months, Warner-Lambert and Wal-Mart began to see the results of their collaborative efforts. Forecast accuracy improved significantly and so did service performance level. No longer did Wal-Mart's buyer threaten Warner-Lambert with the "98 percent in stock or else" consequence. In a turnaround that Nearnberg could not have imagined on that spring day in 1995 when he met with the Wal-Mart buyer, Warner-Lambert was named Wal-Mart's Vendor of the Year in 1996.

Warner-Lambert reaped other benefits from its collaborative efforts with Wal-Mart. The company piloted Wal-Mart's co-managed replenishment process along with three strategic Wal-Mart suppliers. Warner-Lambert was also chosen to be the pilot company for proving the feasibility of developing an industry standard for CPFR®.

During the efforts to develop the collaborative demand planning and co-managed replenishment process, Warner-Lambert came to the same conclusion as Wal-Mart. Technology was needed to enable the process. Otherwise, it was not possible for each supplier to review forecasts of hundreds and thousands of items, provide their market information and recommended changes to the forecasts, and then for Wal-Mart to adjust the forecasts.

It also became obvious that the role and behavior of suppliers' salespeople needed to change to support a collaborative business model. The orientation could not just be pushing product into the customers' stores and distribution centers. The salespeople needed to understand how some of their actions contributed to the bullwhip effect and, in the end, eroded their companies' profit margins.

One destructive and common practice was for salespeople to push for an increase in retailer product orders, even when consumer demand did not reflect the need for an increase. More often than not, what triggered the push was the desire by salespeople and their companies to meet sales revenue targets at month end, quarter end, and end of the year.

This is a common practice throughout industry. Salespeople, with or without their companies' consent, frequently offer price reductions on products to boost sales revenue. These arrangements are negotiated with buyers and the plans are usually not incorporated in the customers' planning and replenishment systems.

By pushing product into customers' distribution centers, the individual salesperson receives a bonus for hitting his or her sales quota and companies avoid criticism by Wall Street analysts. The retailer benefits from the lowered purchase price, but warehousing costs deplete this savings.

While the salesperson and buyer may be happy with this arrangement, the problem is what happens to the rest of the supply chain. A bullwhip effect results. To manufacture product for the bogus demand, overtime for both production and logistics is usually needed. Plus, there are increased freight costs to obtain raw material and ship finished product on short notice.

The bullwhip effect impacts the manufacturing plants and personnel as well. Products that were being replenished at a consistent weekly volume are not ordered for weeks at a time. At times, plant workers have been temporarily laid off when factories become idle.

The supplier's gain is pyrrhic. Profit margins have been traded for meeting a revenue target. While the company achieved a goal, it has reduced the amount of cash flowing into its coffers. Gillette's CEO, Jim Kilts, calls this practice of trade loading the "cycle of doom."*

The CFAR pilot between Warner-Lambert and Wal-Mart illuminated the need to stop the practice of trade loading. Warner-Lambert changed its sales incentive program to reinforce its intention to smooth the bullwhip effect in the Wal-Mart supply chain. Three new metrics were added: point-of-sale forecast accuracy, at the store/item level, as measured against the plan in Retail Link; store service levels; and inventory performance. These additional metrics served to create better alignment of goals and incentives throughout the Warner-Lambert organization. Sales revenue metrics still remained, but now the goal of the sales organization was to better plan for making the sales goals instead of creating last-minute unplanned orders that caused a bullwhip effect and eroded profit margins.

These additional performance metrics provided a more balanced approach to measuring sales performance and proved to be invaluable in the CFAR pilot.

---

* Brooker, Katrina, Jim Kilts is an old-school curmudgeon: nothing could be better for Gillette, *Fortune,* December 17, 2002.

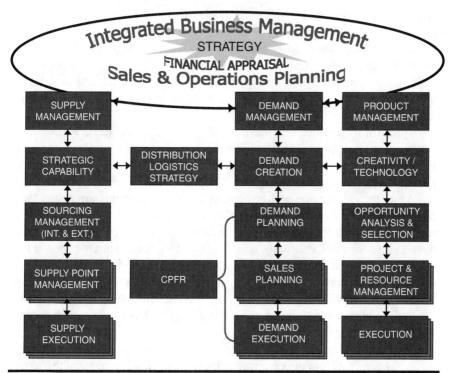

Figure 13. Closed-Loop Enterprise Resource Planning II Process. (©2004 Oliver Wight International.)

Both Wal-Mart and its suppliers, including Warner-Lambert, soon realized how well these metrics indicated the state of the bullwhip effect. When suppliers are tempted to offer month-end or quarter-end deals, or when the buyer waits for a deal before placing orders, the store-level forecast accuracy and inventory-level metrics demonstrate the impact of such decisions.

While Warner-Lambert participated in the pilot programs on co-managed replenishment and CFAR, the need for effective internal planning and collaboration processes became apparent. Many people do not realize that the foundation of CFAR and the resulting VICS industry standard, CPFR®, was based on enterprise resource planning (ERP) principles (see Figure 13). The closed-loop ERP process starts with sales and operations planning to align demand and supply at an aggregate level with a company's strategies and tactics over at least an eighteen-month planning horizon. The demand plan drives the sales and operations planning process. The approved synchronized demand and supply plans are converted into detailed plans that drive sales and marketing execution as well as supply execution.

Realizing the gains that could be made by integrating supply planning with demand collaboration, Warner-Lambert's master scheduler was invited to one of the CFAR pilot meetings with Wal-Mart. When asked the impact on Warner-Lambert's supply organization of improving forecast accuracy by 20 percent, the master scheduler was hard-pressed to answer. Why? Demand plans were converted from aggregate to an SKU level as part of Warner-Lambert's normal planning process. However, the detailed demand plans were not further disaggregated by customer account. Therefore, by the master scheduler's own admission, the supply organization reacted very well to customer-specific emergencies, but did not plan as effectively customer by customer. This was not an unusual situation for a mass-market consumer products company.

The desire to create more accurate forecasts of customer-specific demand was a transformational strategy for Warner-Lambert. It would cause demand and supply organizations to manage their planning and execution differently. It would require a more balanced set of metrics that demonstrated the value of smoothing the bullwhip effect in the supply chain.

It would also require more than just one Warner-Lambert customer to develop similar collaborative planning processes. To optimize the manufacturing and procurement process, Warner-Lambert needed a "critical mass" of retailers to implement demand collaboration processes. Thus, the importance and the need for an industry standard emerged.

Now for the cautionary tale as part of the Warner-Lambert story that was promised at the beginning of this chapter. In implementing any change in a company, the challenge is to stay focused. Especially when changes take many months or years to accomplish, other occurrences can intervene that delay or abort the development of supply chain collaboration. Some of the intervening occurrences are within corporate management's control; others are not.

In the case of Warner-Lambert, two significant diversions occurred that delayed realizing the full potential of the supply chain collaboration effort. The first diversion was the implementation of ERP software. The ERP software took several years to install fully and consumed many company resources, including those people engaged in the supply chain collaboration effort as part of the Y2K effort. (This is a common tussle for companies seeking to implement supply chain collaboration. On the one hand, effective internal planning processes are needed to fully internalize customer demand information throughout the enterprise. On the other hand, the tools required to enable the process can be time consuming to implement and drain company resources in doing so.)

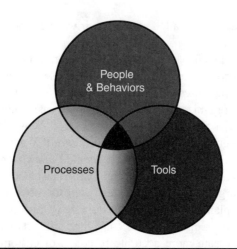

Figure 14. Three Critical Elements of Any Initiative. (©2004 Oliver Wight International.)

For any company initiative, there are three elements that cannot be neglected and must work in concert: process development, people skill development, and enabling technology (see Figure 14). For Warner-Lambert's supply chain collaboration effort, the ERP implementation created a conflict of resources to support the effort. This lengthened the time to realize the benefit from the supply chain collaboration, but ultimately did not stop the process from being developed.

Even though the distraction and resource drain caused by the ERP implementation disappointed Warner-Lambert's collaboration team, the supply chain collaboration effort provided a foundation for utilizing Wal-Mart's retail information in Warner-Lambert's planning processes. The ERP implementation may have prevented expanding the collaboration effort with other retailers, but it still enabled Warner-Lambert to improve its service to Wal-Mart, which represented a significant percentage of annual sales revenues for the company.

The second diversion, which can be much harder to adapt to in a collaborative environment, was Warner-Lambert's acquisition by Pfizer. With the acquisition, roles, responsibilities, and focus within Warner-Lambert shifted under the Pfizer umbrella, affecting the relationship and interaction with Wal-Mart.

To Pfizer's credit, the company's management recognized Warner-Lambert's strengths. They identified Warner-Lambert's collaboration process and organization, as well as the sales organization's orientation for supporting the collaboration effort. This structure survives today.

Why Warner-Lambert's experience is a powerful story is because it illustrates what a company can do to improve its service and financial performance through collaborating with trading partners. It also illustrates the real-world diversions that threaten the continuity of such arrangements. Until supply chain collaboration becomes a standard practice in industry, not just a best practice, continuity will continue to be threatened when significant changes occur within a trading partner organization.

QUESTIONS

1. What was the supply chain collaboration between Wal-Mart and Warner-Lambert called?
2. What were some of the lessons learned from the Wal-Mart/Warner-Lambert Listerine® pilot?
3. What changes were incorporated for the sales organization at Warner-Lambert?
4. What is Wal-Mart's private exchange called?
5. What is "critical mass"?
6. What are the three critical elements to any initiative?

AN INDUSTRY STANDARD FOR SUPPLY CHAIN COLLABORATION

As Wal-Mart, Procter & Gamble, Warner-Lambert, Kimberly-Clark, Johnson & Johnson, Sara Lee, Fruit of the Loom, and Clorox, to name a few of the pioneering companies, developed their supply collaboration processes, one challenge became clear: Maximum benefits could not be gained unless a large number of retailers and suppliers adopted supply chain collaboration as well. Suppliers, in particular, could not realize enough benefits to make the process worthwhile with just one or two retailers as collaborative trading partners. Critical mass, defined as 50 to 60 percent of the retailer companies, was needed.

Critical mass participation alone would not provide the gains manufacturers needed to maximize the benefit from supply chain collaboration, however. There needed to be some consistency in process, practices, and technology data formats among their retail customers and raw material suppliers.

The question was: What is the best way to gain critical mass and consistency in supply chain collaboration processes, practices, and tools? The answer came from a visionary leader with the stature to influence an industry and leverage cooperative industry organizations that already existed.

The leader was Randy Mott, CIO of Wal-Mart at that time, who has since become the CIO of Dell Computer, another company that built its business model and success on a superior supply chain. Mott was (and still is) different from many CIOs of the time. He viewed the role of the CIO as being a catalyst for business innovation and business performance improvement.*

In 1996, Mott served on the board of directors of an independent retail industry standards body, the Voluntary Interindustry Commerce Standards (VICS) Association, whose members included companies from food, apparel, and consumer goods industries. VICS had sponsored several industry standards in recent years, including standards governing electronic data interchange, returns, and advanced ship notices.

Mott believed that VICS was the appropriate organization to develop industry standards for supply chain collaboration or what was known as collaborative forecasting and replenishment (CFAR) at the time. With its broad membership and track record in developing industry standards, the VICS organization had the proven ability to bring together retailers and suppliers to adopt standards in an orderly fashion. This would help to ensure that the standards could be developed faster than forming another standards association for the task.

Mott engaged Robert Bruce, Vice President of Wal-Mart's supply chain, in the effort. With Bruce's industry contacts, he had the ability to reach out to other retailers, consumer goods manufacturers, and technology providers. Some of the retailers and manufacturers he sought out included Target, JC Penney, Procter & Gamble, Nabisco, Sara Lee, Warner-Lambert, Circuit City, Corning, Eastman Kodak, Federated Department Stores, Fieldcrest Cannon, Kimberly-Clark, Kmart, Levi Strauss, Pillsbury, Schnuck Markets, Staples, Philips Consumer Communications, Mead Consumer & Office Products, QRS, and Hewlett-Packard. He also contacted a handful of software providers, including SAP, Syncra, JDA, i2, and Manugistics. Bruce also enlisted the support of consultants from Benchmarking Partners and Ernst & Young to help facilitate and document the agreed-upon standards.

This team initially met in the fall of 1996, renamed CFAR to CPFR® in order to add the term "planning" to the collaboration process, and by early 1997 the VICS CPFR® Working Group was officially sponsored as an independent industry body for supply chain collaboration standards.

The CPFR® Working Group, with Bruce as chairman and Joe Andraski shortly afterward partnering with him as co-chairman, quickly expanded its membership and participation by members (see Figure 15). These companies joined forces to develop what is known today as the CPFR® Guidelines.

It is worthwhile to review how the CPFR® Guidelines were developed. This can help other industries to adopt similar guidelines through adaptation rather

---

* Wilder, Clinton, Chief of Year: Wal-Mart CIO Randy Mott innovates for his company's — and customer's — good, *Information Week,* December 22, 1997.

Accenture
ACCO Brands
Ace Hardware
Arrow Electronics
Best Buy Company
Cambridge Towel
Campbell Soup Co.
Circuit City Stores
ConAgra Frozen Foods
Corning Consumer Products Co.
Crowe, Chizek & Company
DAMA Project Demantra
Deluxe Video
E3 Corporation
Eastman Kodak
Edgewood Consulting Group
Efficient Market Services
e.Intelligence, Inc.
Electronic Arts
E-Millennium
Ernst & Young LLP
EXE Technologies
Extricity
Federated Dept. Stores
Fieldcrest Cannon, Inc./ Pillowtex
Food Distributors International
Food Marketing Institute
Garan
Georgia Pacific Corp.
GFT (Apparel)
Gillette
GlobalNetXchange
Golden Books
H.E. Butt Grocery Company
Hershey Foods
Hewlett-Packard Corporation
HON Company
i2 Technologies
IBM

IPNET Solutions
Jack Haedicke & Associates
JCPenney Co., Inc.
Johnson & Johnson
Johnsonville Sausage LLC
Kellogg's
KhiMetrics
Kimberly-Clark Corporation
Kmart Corporation
Kraft Foods, Inc.
Kurt Salmon Associates
LakeWest Group
Lawrence Livermore Nat'l Labs
Levi Strauss & Co.
Logility
Lucent Technologies
Manco
Manugistics
Mars, Inc.
Marshall Field's
Mead School & Office Products
Meijer, Inc.
Microsoft Corporation
Milliken & Company
Milton Merl Associates
Motorola
Nabisco, Inc.
NCR Corporation
Nestlé
Newell Rubbermaid
Nonstop Solutions
Northwestern University
Novopoint
Ocean Spray Cranberries
Oliver Wight
OMI
Oracle
Pharmavite Corporation
Pillsbury Company, The
Playtex Products

Prestone
Prevo's Family Markets
PricewaterhouseCoopers
Procter & Gamble Co.
QRS Corporation
Ralston Purina
Retail Council of Canada
Retek, Inc.
Safeway
Sam's Club
San Diego State University
Sara Lee Corporation
Schering-Plough
Schnuck Markets, Inc.
Service Merchandise
Sherwin-Williams
Shopko Stores
Staples
Strategy 3D
Sure Fit, Inc.
Surgency (formerly Benchmarking Partners)
Syncra Systems
Target Corp.
Textile Clothing Technologies
ThinkFast Consulting
Thomson Consumer Electronics
Toastmaster
Transora
TUMI Software
Uniform Code Council
Unilever
Uniteq Application Viewlocity
VF Corporation
Walgreen's
Wal-Mart Stores, Inc.
Warner-Lambert Co.
Wolf Camera
Worldwide Dreams
World Wide Retail Exchange

Figure 15. Companies Participating in the VICS CPFR® Effort. (©2004 Oliver Wight International.)

Change the relationship paradigm between trading partners and create significantly more accurate information that can drive the value chain to greater sales and profits.

Figure 16. VICS CPFR® Subcommittee Mission Statement. (©2004 Oliver Wight International.)

than "reinventing the wheel." For example, the Supply Chain Council SCOR Model adopted the CPFR® Guidelines, based on the VICS approach, in 2004.*

The first order of business for the newly formed VICS CPFR® Working Group was to agree on a mission statement. The mission statement (Figure 16) was important because the mission was not just to develop a standard. Rather, the early members of the working group recognized the underlying purpose of the effort in the mission statement, and that purpose was to bring about financial benefits — greater sales and profits — to trading partners.

Next, the team established guiding principles for the working group, which was important in defining the scope of the effort (see Figure 17). As you can see from the principles, the team realized that more than a technology industry standard for interoperability was needed. Standard guidelines for the collaborative business processes were needed as well. In fact, the content of the current industry standard is 80 percent business process guidelines and 20 percent technology standards.

In developing the CPFR® standards, it was fascinating to see how a group of competitors worked together so productively. The fact that customers and suppliers, technology providers, and consultants formed such an effective team illustrates the strong belief that the effort was right for the industry. A passion for the purpose of supply chain collaboration remains today as the VICS CPFR®

* Supply Chain Council, www.supply-chain.org.

- Joint business planning
- Common goals and metrics
- Agreement to collaborate
- Use technology standards for data sharing
  - Data, text, and security
- Measurement and reporting of joint benefits and performance results

Figure 17. VICS CPFR® Guiding Principles. (©2004 Oliver Wight International.)

work continues, particularly in documenting the results from CPFR® efforts and providing a forum for developing more detailed definitions and models for supply chain collaboration.

Over the years, VICS CPFR® subcommittees have been formed and the Uniform Code Council (UCC) has added its sponsorship to the effort. The subcommittees are developing guidelines for business process best practices, metrics, technology, n-Tier — for multiple trading partner collaboration, collaborative warehousing, and marketing. The team has also expanded globally to Europe, Asia, and South America.

Other industries standards bodies have joined the VICS CPFR® group. These bodies include the high-technology industry's RosettaNet and the apparel industry's DAMA. In addition, the academic community is extremely interested in the efforts being put forth by the CPFR® team and many universities now participate in the VICS CPFR® sessions.

What emerged from the VICS effort are guidelines for implementing CPFR®.* These guidelines address process flow as well as roles and responsibilities involved in each of the nine steps in the CPFR® process. A summary of the nine steps is shown in Figure 18 and a process flow for one business scenario is shown in Figure 19.

Based on my experience in helping to develop the CPFR® guidelines and in helping companies to implement supply chain collaboration, an overview of each step in a supply collaboration process can be seen in Figures 20 through 28. The overviews are based on the structure defined in the VICS CPFR® guidelines. The purpose of each step is highlighted and the activities that occur in each step are summarized. These step-by-step overviews are intended to help you structure a supply chain collaboration process with your trading partners.

---

* CPFR® Voluntary Guidelines, Voluntary Interindustry Commerce Standards Association, 1998.

Step 1: Front-End Arrangement
  – Agree to confidentiality and dispute resolutions
  – Develop scorecard to track supply chain metrics
  – Establish incentives

Step 2: Joint Business Plan
  – Partners develop plans for promotions,
    inventory policy changes, new product introductions,
    store openings and closings

Steps 3 to 5: Sales Forecast Collaboration
  – Trading partners share demand forecasts and identify
    exceptions. Collaboration on causal factors to reach
    consensus on a single forecast number.

Steps 6 to 8: Order Forecast Collaboration
  – Trading partners share replenishment plans and
    identify and resolve exceptions.

Step 9: Order Generation/Delivery Execution
  – Execution results data are shared and forecast
    accuracy problems are reviewed. Performance metrics
    are reported and communicated.

Figure 18. Summary of Nine Steps in the VICS CPFR® Guidelines.

It is important to remember that the VICS CPFR® Nine-Step Standard and my overview based on that standard are guidelines. How companies execute supply chain collaboration and the extent to which the processes yield a competitive and financial advantage depend on how companies decide to operate the processes. For Procter & Gamble and other companies, supply chain collaboration was part of their firms' transformational strategies. Other companies implement parts of supply chain collaboration to meet perceived or mandated expectations from their companies and do not intend to utilize it to significantly improve their financial and competitive performance.

As a result, some companies, particularly those that see supply chain collaboration as a transformational effort, utilize all nine steps of the process. Others adopt only a few steps. Still others will start by adopting a few steps and take an evolutionary approach to employing all of the supply chain collaboration processes.

Other factors in determining how fully to implement supply chain collaboration are a company's internal planning competency and capabilities, a company's trading partners' capabilities, and the types of products and the market in which supply chains operate. The point is that every company will approach adopting supply chain collaboration in a different way.

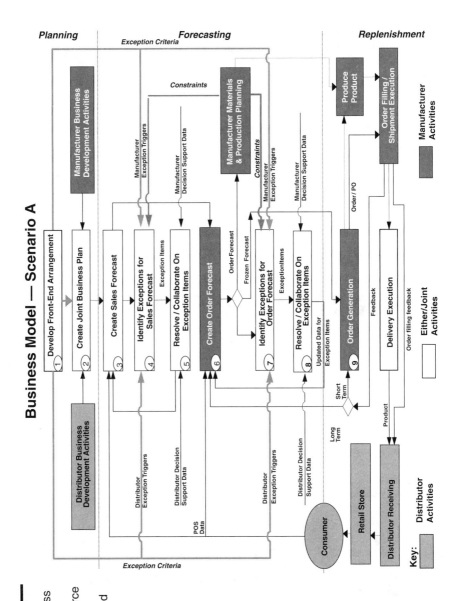

Figure 19.
VICS CPFR® Business Model. (© Voluntary Interindustry Commerce Standards [VICS] Association. Reprinted with permission.)

Step 1: Front-End Arrangement

Purpose:
Establish rules and guidelines for a collaborative relationship.

Summary:
Teach each partner the business process and agree on points of collaboration.

Result:
Document who does what, when, and how.

Process Steps:
1. Develop Mission Statement
   - Shared understanding and objectives
   - Confidentiality
   - Empowerment
2. Determine Goals and Objectives
   - Define opportunity
   - Define common metrics
   - Define impacts to each partner's business
3. Discuss Competencies, Resources, and Systems
   - Determine each partner's strengths and capabilities
4. Define Collaboration Points and Responsible Business Functions
   - Determine how each functional group performs collaboration, including the timing of the collaboration
5. Determine Information Sharing Needs
   - Outline information to be shared
   - Determine frequency of information sharing
   - Determine technology required to enable information sharing
6. Determine Service and Order Commitments
   - Agree on desired service levels and time frames that represent an order commitment
7. Determine Resource Involvement and Commitments
   - Determine the staffing needed to support the process, including time commitments
8. Define Conflict Resolution Process
   - Agree on rules for identifying and resolving disagreements
9. Determine Process for Reviewing the Collaborative Arrangement
   - Establish ongoing evaluation process
   - Determine how the success of the relationship will be benchmarked and reported
   - Determine when formal reviews will be conducted and who will participate in the reviews
10. Publish Front-End Arrangement
    - Publish and distribute the front-end arrangement to senior executives and participants in the collaboration process

Figure 20. Front-End Arrangement Process Overview. (©2004 Oliver Wight International.)

Step 2: Joint Business Plan

Purpose:
Exchange information about corporate strategies, business plans, promotions and events, and other activities that will influence consumer demand and product availability.

Summary:
Understand each partner's needs and capabilities in creating and influencing demand, manufacturing product, and replenishing product.

Result:
Flow chart of process roles and rules for managing the collaboration process from forecasting through manufacturing and replenishment.

Process Steps:
1. Identify Partner Strategies
   - Share information about business goals, strategies, and objectives
2. Develop Category Roles, Objectives, and Goals
   - Discuss each partner's objectives by product category
   - Determine each partner's role and function in the collaborative process by category
3. Develop Joint Category Strategies and Tactics
   - Identify appropriate category strategies for promotions, pricing, marketing, and new item launches
4. Develop Item Management Profiles
   - Define item rules, including order minimums, lead times, order intervals, time zones that represent an order commitment, and safety stock targets
5. Develop Joint Business Plan
   - Define individual actions in support of the defined goals and objectives for each partner by functional areas of responsibility
6. Agree to Joint Business Plan
   - Review the joint business plan to ensure alignment with each trading partner's strategic and tactical goals and objectives
   - Review the joint business plan with the front-end arrangement to ensure alignment

Figure 21.   Joint Business Plan Process Overview. (©2004 Oliver Wight International.)

Step 3: Demand Forecast Creation

Purpose:
Create a sales demand forecast that will lead to the creation of the replenishment supply order by the retailer/customer.

Summary:
The consumer demand forecast is the starting place for collaboration. Forecasted consumer demand can be represented at the store/shelf level, distribution center, or corporate level.

Result:
A consensus forecast of demand that is agreed on by both trading partners.

Process Steps:
1. Analyze Joint Business Plan
   - Assess how the forecast is to be created, according to the joint business plan, including timing of the communication, how the forecast will be generated, how feedback will be provided, and how consensus will be reached on the forecast
2. Analyze Causal Factors
   - Determine the impact of seasonality, promotions, and other causal factors that impact demand patterns
   - Determine how adjustments will be made based on causal factors
3. Collect and Analyze Point-of-Sale History
   - Utilize point-of-sale history (or warehouse withdrawal information if point-of-sale history is not available) to generate a forecast of base demand volume
   - Exclude nonrepeatable events from the historical data
4. Identify Planned Events
   - Create and share an event calendar of planned activities that will impact demand, including store openings and closings, new items, and promotions
5. Identify Exceptions or Forecast Disagreements
   - Identify when the proposed forecast significantly differs from past history. Validate that the forecast is correct.
   - Identify disagreements with the forecast and collaborate on resolving the disagreements
6. Generate the Demand Forecast
   - Apply all causal and exception adjustments to the base forecast
   - Communicate the forecast to the parties/functions agreed on in the joint business plan, using the technology agreed on to do so

Figure 22.   Demand Forecast Creation Process Overview. (©2004 Oliver Wight International.)

Step 4: Identify Item-Level Exceptions to the Demand Forecast

Purpose:
Identify item-level forecast exceptions, based on pre-established tolerances defined in the front-end arrangement and joint business plan. (When hundreds and thousands of items are being planned, a technology tool is required to perform this analysis.)

Summary:
Using pre-established tolerances and metrics, identify exceptions in the demand forecast for collaborative resolution by the partners.

Result:
Forecast exceptions are identified, usually by the technology tool when hundreds and thousands of items are being planned. The exceptions are communicated to the appropriate functional people for both trading partners. Discussion and judgment results in a collaborative decision about the demand forecast in question.

Process Steps:
1. Understand and Retrieve Exception Criteria
   - Obtain exception criteria agreed on in the front-end arrangement and joint business plan
   - Input the exception criteria into the technology tool
2. Identify Changes and Updates
   - Review the exception criteria and update any agreed on changes to the criteria in the technology tool
3. Update the System with the Constrained Demand Forecast
   - Based on decisions made during the sales and operations planning process, adjust the demand forecast accordingly
4. Compare Item Values to Exception Criteria
   - Record the exception gap opportunity where forecast accuracy differs from the accuracy goal
5. Identify Exceptions for Collaboration
   - Discuss causes for the gap in performance by item and agree on actions that need to be taken

Figure 23. Process Overview for Identifying Item-Level Exceptions to the Demand Forecast. (©2004 Oliver Wight International.)

Step 5: Collaborate and Resolve Demand Forecast Exception Items

Purpose:
Resolve exceptions to the demand forecast through trading partner collaboration.

Summary:
Use communications process to communicate the exceptions, provide supporting information that will aid in resolving the exceptions, and communicate the resolution agreed on.

Result:
Identify adjustments to the demand forecast.

Process Steps:
1. Identify Desired Adjustments to the Demand Forecast
   - Determine proposed adjustments to the appropriate functions for collaboration and consensus
2. Recommend Forecast Adjustments
   - Recommend and communicate proposed forecast adjustments
   - Validate that the proposed forecast adjustments are aligned with the front-end arrangement and joint business plan
3. Agree on the Forecast Adjustments
   - Reach agreement on the proposed adjustments
   - If agreement cannot be reached, utilize the conflict resolution process defined in the front-end arrangement to reach a decision
   - Update the demand forecast in the planning tool and communicate the demand forecast to the replenishment planning function

---

Figure 24. Process Overview for Collaborating and Resolving Demand Forecast Exception Items. (©2004 Oliver Wight International.)

For example, some companies develop a front-end arrangement (Step 1 in the VICS CPFR® Guidelines). In my experience, those companies that develop a front-end arrangement as part of the trading partner relationship tend to develop better win/win relationships than those that do not. Some front-end arrangements are very simple: a one- or two-page document that outlines the objective, desired mutual benefit, and how the companies must interact to realize the benefit. Other companies opt for a front-end arrangement that is a legal and contractually binding document. The Appendix shows a generic front-end arrangement developed as part of the VICS CPFR® Guidelines. This document can be used as a starting point for developing your own front-end arrangement.

While 80 percent of the guidelines address process, companies should not neglect the technology standards that have been developed. The VICS CPFR® Working Group has published data models and XML standards for technology

Step 6: Create the Replenishment Order Forecast

Purpose:
Develop and communicate a time-phased projection of replenishment orders based on the demand forecast.

Summary:
Use the demand forecast (which is based on point-of-sale history and causal factors), inventory strategies, and joint business plan objectives to create a replenishment order forecast.

Result:
A time-phased replenishment order forecast.

Process Steps:
1. Communicate the Demand Forecast (which was developed based on point-of-sale history, seasonality, promotions and other causal factors)
2. Consider Inventory Strategies and Current Inventory Levels
   - Review inventory strategies
   - Determine current inventory levels, including on-hand, on-order, and in-transit inventory
3. Analyze the Manufacturer's Historical Replenishment Performance
   - Review fill rates, on-time delivery, and other metrics that determine replenishment performance
4. Analyze and Communicate Manufacturing Capacity Limitations
   - Communicate capacity limitations that could impact replenishment capability over the near term and longer term
5. Evaluate Factors Affecting Replenishment Planning Decisions
   - Review lead times, time zones agreed on for order commitments, and other factors and tactics
6. Review Execution Performance
   - Review order filling and shipment execution performance
7. Create Order Replenishment Forecast
   - Based on the above, generate the order replenishment forecast

Figure 25. Process Overview for Creating the Replenishment Order Forecast. (©2004 Oliver Wight International.)

that enable and automate supply chain collaboration.* By utilizing technology tools that conform to these standards, the automated exchange of data between partners becomes consistent and redundant tools are not needed to execute supply chain collaboration with multiple trading partners. The Global Commerce Initiative (GCI) has also endorsed the VICS CPFR® technology guide-

---

* CPFR® Voluntary Guidelines, Voluntary Interindustry Commerce Standards Association, 1998.

Step 7: Identify Exceptions to the Order Replenishment Forecast

Purpose:
Identify replenishment orders, based on pre-established tolerances and criteria.

Summary:
Determine item-level order forecasts that should be reviewed and validated, based on pre-established tolerances and criteria identified in the front-end arrangement and joint business plan.

Result:
Develop a list of exceptions to review collaboratively between trading partners.

Process Steps:
1. Understand and Retrieve Exception Criteria
   - Obtain exception criteria agreed on in the front-end arrangement and joint business plan
   - Keep the exception criteria up to date in the technology tool
2. Utilize the Replenishment Order Forecast in the Sales and Operations Planning Process
   - Identify manufacturer's recommended changes to the replenishment order forecast
   - Identify distributors' recommended changes to the replenishment order forecast
3. Compare the Proposed Replenishment Order Forecast to Supply and Capacity
   - Determine supply and capacity constraints
   - Determine supply and capacity optimization opportunities
4. Apply Constraints and Capacity Optimization Factors to the Order Replenishment Forecast
   - Create a revised order replenishment forecast
5. Identify Exceptions Items
   - Identify exception items based on the pre-established tolerances and criteria

---

Figure 26.   Process Overview for Identifying Exceptions to the Order Replenishment Forecast. (©2004 Oliver Wight International.)

lines and standards, which means that the same guidelines and standards are available for global trading partners.

We expect supply chain collaboration guidelines and standards to evolve, change, and be updated over time. In fact, at the time of this writing, the VICS CPFR® Working Group is enhancing the current nine-step model to be more interactive versus sequential (see Figure 29). We expect other industries to develop guidelines as well. The value of the standards is to help trading partners more quickly pilot supply chain collaboration and then adapt and improve the process based on their pilot experiences. In the next chapter, we will review the early successes and failures of supply chain collaboration.

Step 8: Collaborate and Resolve Exceptions to the Order Replenishment Forecast

Purpose:
Resolve exceptions to the order replenishment forecast through trading partner collaboration.

Summary:
Use communications process to communicate exceptions, provide supporting information that will aid in resolving the exceptions, and communicate the resolution agreed on.

Result:
Identify adjustments to the order replenishment forecast.

Process Steps:
1. Identify and Communicate Exceptions, Along with Supporting Information
2. Recommend Order Replenishment Forecast Adjustments
   - Recommend and communicate proposed forecast adjustments
   - Validate that the proposed forecast adjustments are aligned with the front-end arrangement and joint business plan
3. Agree on the Forecast Adjustments
   - Reach agreement on the proposed adjustments
   - If agreement cannot be reached, utilize the conflict resolution process defined in the front-end arrangement to reach a decision
   - Update the planning system with the adjustments

Figure 27. Process Overview for Collaborating and Resolving Exceptions to the Order Replenishment Forecast. (©2004 Oliver Wight International.)

Step 9: Create the Replenishment Order

Purpose:
Create and communicate the replenishment order.

Summary:
Execute the replenishment order based on the collaborative replenishment order forecast agreed on.

Result:
Replenishment orders that are in sync with the demand forecast and are aligned with the joint business plan.

Process Steps:
1. Utilize the Planning System to Generate and Communicate Replenishment Orders Internally and to the Trading Partner

Figure 28. Create the Replenishment Order Process Overview. (©2004 Oliver Wight International.)

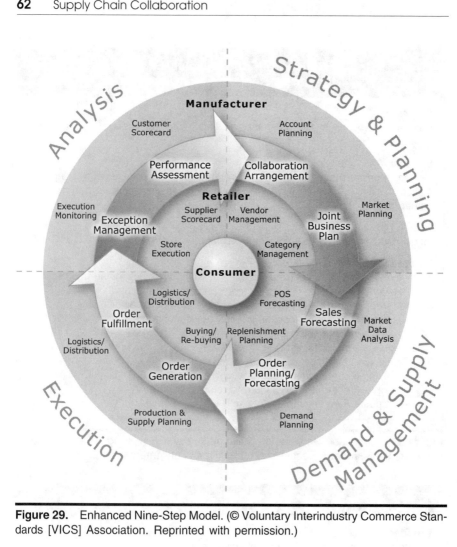

Figure 29.   Enhanced Nine-Step Model. (© Voluntary Interindustry Commerce Standards [VICS] Association. Reprinted with permission.)

QUESTIONS

1. Why is critical mass important?
2. How does a supply chain collaboration standard help trading partners?
3. What is VICS and what does it do?
4. What are the two primary types of standards for CPFR®?
5. Why are the VICS CPFR® standards called guidelines?

6

EARLY WINS
AND FAILURES

Hundreds of companies have implemented some form of supply chain collaboration over the years. The majority of these implementations have occurred in the retail industry, although the high-technology sector has utilized supply chain collaboration as well.

The use of supply chain collaboration has yielded learning, both good and bad. No matter how well an implementation is planned, it is inevitable that something new will be discovered when it is actually executed. The purpose of this chapter is to discuss early wins and failures so that you will know what to expect and what to avoid, if possible.

Our advice, however, is to not to overstudy supply chain collaboration. In the words of the popular Nike advertisements, "Just do it." David Glass, former president and CEO of Wal-Mart and current member of the board of directors, was well known for his statement, "If you want to lose your job at Wal-Mart, form a committee and study something." The longer that companies delay in implementing supply chain collaboration, the longer they delay realizing the financial and partner relationships from collaboration.

We find that too many companies suffer from "analysis paralysis." Too many companies try to make sure they know everything before they are willing to act. The fact is, we cannot know everything. It is more important to act and then adapt as needed, learning from successes and failures.

A speaker at a conference many years ago told his audience, "If you are able to learn from your mistakes, you just need to make your mistakes faster." This approach has enabled many companies to drive far ahead of their competitors in realizing the benefits from supply chain collaboration.

The fact is, no matter how much we study supply chain collaboration, the best way to really learn it is to do it. It is amazing how many companies have never missed a VICS CPFR® Working Group meeting and yet are still studying it to see if their own company should implement a pilot to test the waters. I call this behavior squandered opportunity.

Many people do not know that Procter & Gamble's first foray into supply chain management was with Kmart. Procter & Gamble tested a prototype of automated continuous replenishment with Wal-Mart's archrival. The pilot was successful in significantly reducing acquisition costs for diapers. The effort was seen by Kmart's executives as a distribution project, however. Procter & Gamble used the Kmart pilot as a proving ground. It has since expanded collaboration using continuous replenishment to all of its key customers and is widely recognized for its pioneering role in developing the processes for CPFR®.

In starting with its pioneering efforts, Procter & Gamble did not envision that supply chain collaboration would evolve to where it is today. Ralph Drayer, Procter & Gamble's Vice President of Customer Service and Logistics at the time, observes:

> When we started this whole customer business development team and extending our supply chain work beyond the four walls of P&G, we knew that there was value there, but we kind of learned as we went. We did not know that it would end up serving as a foundation for a vastly improved trading relationship.*

Procter & Gamble's experience is not unique. The lesson is this: Companies should assess the risk of doing and not doing supply chain collaboration. The risk of not developing supply chain collaboration as a competency is falling behind your competitors. This certainly proved true with Kmart, which chose not to expand its supply chain collaboration effort with Procter & Gamble beyond the pilot stage, even though the pilot had been highly successful.* Kmart ended up declaring bankruptcy while Wal-Mart has ended up as the undisputed, most successful retailer in the world.

No matter when you start supply chain collaboration, now or later, you will experience early wins and failures as you develop the processes and competencies. So what have been some of the early wins and failures? Figure 1 in Chapter 1 showed CPFR® pilot results compiled in a survey conducted by AMR Research. The survey shows improvements in sales revenue and reductions in inventory as some of the benefits of CPFR®.

---

* Koch, Christopher, It all began with Drayer, *CIO*, August 1, 2002.

What the survey did not show was how much forecast accuracy was improved. In the many collaboration efforts we have been involved with, forecast accuracy has improved from 20 to 40 percent and even more so for products on promotion. Why do we emphasize forecast accuracy? Without improved forecast accuracy, it is very difficult to dampen the bullwhip effect.

Improved forecast accuracy alone, however, does not ensure that the bullwhip effect will be dampened or eliminated. This was proven when analyzing the reasons for early failures. Quite often, the demand forecast is not used in the supply chain execution system and process, primarily in the manufacturer's side of the chain.

Why is the collaborative forecast not used? There can be many reasons. Some companies lack the technology to drive the customer-specific forecast into their planning systems directly. Customer facing teams and salespeople do not communicate the customer forecast, choosing instead to hoard the information. Many times, the forecast is communicated, but is not used because its accuracy is questioned. To sum up, the reasons for not using the customer-generated forecast are people, processes, and technology, in that order.

A supply chain collaboration pilot helps companies to identify strengths and weaknesses in people, processes, and technology. It demonstrates readiness to implement on a wider scale and what is needed to develop the competency and infrastructure to support supply chain collaboration.

The lack of technology does not have to hold companies back. Many supply chain collaboration efforts began with minimal technology support. It is difficult to expand to multiple partners without supporting technology, however. When technology support is nonexistent or limited, companies typically focus first on collaborating with strategic customers that are significant to their current and future growth.

Even efforts that are small in scope have yielded early benefits. One of the most frequently cited early wins in collaboration comes from sharing common information and reaching consensus on a plan. When information is shared and validated, confusion and errors can be avoided. Time and energy can be much better spent focused on the end customer or consumer.

Many companies have utilized the sharing of information to prevent errors and identify potential problems. Companies use various methods to detect potential errors, some even going so far as to hire hourly people to monitor the data shared by retailers and look for errors and potential irregularities.

What types of errors and problems do partners look for? Errors range from incorrect item classification to wrong lead times to products inactivated by the system incorrectly. An early win for Warner-Lambert was identifying a demand aggregation disconnect with Wal-Mart. In comparing the store-level forecast to the store rebuying orders communicated to the distribution center, the difference between the two was as high as 300 percent. Because Warner-Lambert had access to the same data as the Wal-Mart replenishment analyst, it was able to resolve this disconnect fairly quickly. The result was smoothing of the bullwhip effect.

Having a common view of the same information between trading partners allows for potential discrepancies and disconnects to be discussed and resolved more effectively (before they become problems). Because both partners are reviewing the same information, wasted time in determining whose data are right is eliminated.

My experience has shown that most companies vastly underestimate the number of errors that occur in execution systems. Even if supply chain collaboration is utilized as narrowly as detecting errors, there are benefits from the effort. Some manufacturers argue, and perhaps rightly so, that they should not have to hire employees to catch retailers' errors. But on the other side of the coin, it is normally the manufacturers who must react to undetected mistakes. So, why not try and prevent the errors in the first place?

Another early win in supply chain collaboration is better serving the end users or consumers. In the retail industry, the point-of-sale demand history and demand forecast are catalysts for better serving consumers. By reviewing this information together and factoring in future plans (such as promotions and new product launches), the demand forecast more accurately reflects reality. More accurate and realistic demand plans are created, which in turn results in improved store in-stock levels and reduced inventory safety stock levels.

A pilot by consumer goods manufacturer Henkel Spain and Spanish retailer Condis resulted in a 15 percent improvement in forecast accuracy. This improvement made possible a sustained customer service level of 99 percent without increasing inventory, even during promotion periods that previously resulted in a high amount of out-of-stocks. During the pilot, the two firms reduced rush orders 6 percent and increased truck fill and pallet fill rates to 99 percent.*

When the demand forecast is tied to the trading partners' execution systems, a more accurate execution system is created, whether it is the retailer's replenishment order system or the manufacturer's production and material requirements planning system. This is what is meant by the term "operating to a single set of numbers." Operating to a single set of numbers has long been considered

---

* Seiffert, Dirk, CPFR®: ready to take off in Europe, in *Collaborative Planning Forecasting and Replenishment: How to Create a Supply Chain Advantage,* Galileo Business, 2002, pp. 191–192.

a best practice in the manufacturing industry. This concept is now being applied throughout supply chains with good results.

When a single demand plan number drives supply chain planning and execution systems, the demand plan becomes the "lifeblood" of the supply chain. All the links in the supply chain are connected by a single demand plan that most accurately reflects true consumer or end user demand, just like the blood vessels connect the brain, heart, organs, and tissue inside of all of us.

If all the supply chain links are connected by the same single forecast of demand, deviations between the forecast and the execution plans at each link can be identified and rationalized. Sometimes, the deviations are a wise choice on the part of a trading partner; many times, the deviations are not even recognized. When they are recognized and rationalized, problems that would result in poor customer service, the production of the wrong mix of products, and unnecessary inventory can be prevented.

Here is an early failure example. A single forecast was used to drive the retailer's and manufacturer's execution systems; however, no one checked for deviations in the forecast of anticipated demand compared to historical demand. An appliance retailer inadvertently inactivated all of the twenty-five-inch color televisions for one manufacturer. The inactivation was to go into effect six months into the future. The appliance retailer's demand forecast reflected the change in demand due to the inactivation. Unfortunately, no one in either the retailer's or manufacturer's organization challenged the change.

Six months later, the retailer did not have twenty-five-inch televisions in stock. It took five days to identify and resolve the problem. It took another two weeks for the televisions to be supplied to the retailer. Both the retailer and manufacturer lost tens of thousands of dollars in sales revenue.

Sure it was the retailer's mistake, but it could have been prevented had anyone in the supply chain compared the demand forecast to historical demand. In this case, collaboration did not occur. The so-called collaboration was merely a transaction between planning and execution systems. Supply chain collaboration is really all about better decision making on behalf of end users and consumers and each trading partner. This cannot be accomplished on autopilot; it requires human interaction and intervention.

Better execution of collaborative decisions is another early win in supply chain collaboration. One could argue that collaboration is not new. Companies have been collaborating since the invention of business. It is important to understand that there are various forms of collaboration. One form is communication. The other form is decision making and the execution of decisions.

Early wins have come from improved communication between trading partners on promotions and other events. Collaboration on promotions entails working together to agree on the timing and determining the expected lift in demand from the promotion. Once this is determined, collaboration goes a step further to ensure that promotion demand is included in the demand forecast. Once it is, then the retailer's replenishment system and manufacturer's planning and execution system should reflect the planned promotion and lift in demand.

One of the early wins from supply chain collaboration is trading partners working together to develop a better understanding of each other's plans. This has led to working together to develop what Ralph Drayer calls superior consumer value. Procter & Gamble ended up changing the name of its sales organization to customer business development to reflect the desire to work with customers to develop mutual ways to create improved consumer value. This is accomplished by working together to develop and execute a joint business plan.

To further emphasize this new strategic approach within Procter & Gamble, according to Drayer, Procter & Gamble eliminated the sales quota of orders. Sales representatives' orientation changed from order takers to making Procter & Gamble's customers more profitable in the product categories supplied by Procter & Gamble. The order transaction became the responsibility of the logistics person on the category team.*

This brings us to one of the most significant early wins. It is known as the people side, or soft side, of the business. Attitudes toward trading partners shift from adversarial to cooperative. In doing so, freedom is gained — freedom to work together to try new things — whether in assortment planning, micromerchandising, promotional management, replenishment, transportation optimization, item file synchronization, or radio frequency identification. We learned at Wal-Mart that when we worked with manufacturers in the above areas, we all managed risk better. We worked together to prevent and identify problems we did not anticipate as early as possible and then worked together to solve the problems. It is hard to classify these types of benefits. Some people explain the win as "having skin in the game."

It has been interesting to note the difference in win/win benefits between CPFR®, which emphasizes trading partner collaboration, and vendor managed inventory, which traditionally has neglected the win/win aspects of collaboration. With traditional vendor managed inventory programs, the retailer takes no ownership for the inventory, inventory decisions, or accountability for its role in creating the inventory via the bullwhip effect and tactical choices.

Some will argue that vendor managed inventory has had some great successes. In our opinion, its shortfall is that the retailer takes no accountability

---

* Koch, Christopher, It all began with Drayer, *CIO*, August 1, 2002.

in the process, rarely assists in the program, and then places all the blame on the supplier when anything goes wrong. In our experience, the bullwhip effect tends to be much greater with vendor managed inventory than in a collaborative partnership.

When both trading partners agree to a win/win collaborative partnership, we have observed that companies' attitudes toward their trading partners change. They leverage one another as if managing an asset. In many cases, companies with collaborative relationships also collaborate in other joint programs, such as assortment planning, micromerchandising, transportation optimization, item file synchronization, promotional management, and radio frequency identification.

In citing the aforementioned early successes of supply chain collaboration, it is also necessary to note the early failures. The cause of most early failures can be summed up in a simple statement: I win, you figure out how to win. When this is the attitude of one partner toward the other, the results will always be disappointing.

The "I win, you figure out how to win" attitude demonstrates that the root cause of most collaboration failures centers around people and processes. Rarely is the technology the fault. What has made trading partner collaboration difficult to execute is the change it requires in attitude, culture, and business models. Corporate culture, roles, responsibilities, and organizational structures usually need to be modified to collaborate successfully with supply chain partners. These changes do not just occur with the selling, buying, and logistics organizations. The needed changes encompass the senior leadership of business enterprises, including the CEO, president, and COO.

Figure 30 documents the most common examples of people and process issues that have caused collaborative efforts to be less than successful.

I have been involved with several collaboration pilots where it was obvious that the pilot was going to fail. In general, if I do not see the retailer's buying organization or the supplier's sales and marketing organizations involved in the pilot, it is a warning signal for failure. Why? Because the actions of the buyer and the sales and marketing organizations can be counterproductive to collaborating in a way in which both business enterprises can derive profits from the effort. Review Figure 30 again. Ask yourself how the buyer's decision to cancel orders to meet his or her personal inventory measurement target impacts the supplier, who most probably has at a minimum purchased the raw material to support the order or is in the process of producing the order. Ask yourself also how the salesperson's decision to make a deal with the retailer to meet his or her sales goal impacts both the supplier and retailer. The supplier makes unneeded product and does so using labor overtime. The retailer purchases product before it needs to and carries the inventory.

Retailer Reasons for Failure	Supplier Reasons for Failure
• Buyer cancels orders at the end of each month in order to meet individual inventory ownership measurements, even at the cost of out of stock.	• Salesperson offers the retail buyer a deal at end of quarter to meet sales revenue objectives, creating additional inventory for the retailer at the cost of expedited freight and overtime. (Salesperson often receives bonus for doing this deal making even though, in many cases, the supplier loses money.)
• Buying organization is not linked to replenishment team function, which is sponsoring the supply chain collaboration program, resulting in unanticipated buyer-generated orders.	• The sales organization is not engaged in the collaboration program as it has no accountability for supply chain activities and company profits.
• Deals and forward buying occur independent of the collaboration effort.	• Poor integration of the retailer demand forecasts into the supplier's demand and supply planning systems, resulting in the supply organization being unprepared to satisfy the demand.
• No accountability for the order forecast and now ownership of the formal forecasting process.	• Lack of sharing information internally on the retailer's planned events and promotions, resulting in unanticipated spikes in demand.
• Internal collaboration within the retailer business enterprise is poor.	• No sales and operations planning process for synchronizing demand and supply — and validating that the demand plan can be fulfilled.
• Lack of trust — both internally and with the trading partner.	• Lack of trust — both internally and with the trading partner.
• Poor execution — not doing what the retailer said it was going to do.	• Poor execution — not doing what the supplier said it was going to do.

Figure 30.   Reasons for Failure.

Recently I was involved with a CPFR® pilot where the early wins were significant. The two trading partners had improved the point-of-sale forecast accuracy from 70 to 92 percent out at the distribution center level that had been aggregated up from store level. The accuracy measurement was based on the forecast thirty days prior. As a result, replenishment orders had been significantly smoothed and were more predictable. It also was discovered that the aggregation of the store demand was incorrect. As a result of improved forecasting, more predictable replenishment orders, and the correction of the aggregation error, store in-stocks improved by 8 percent, safety stocks were reduced from three weeks to one week for the retailer, and the supplier reduced safety stock inventory from six weeks to three weeks. Sales revenue also increased 10 percent.

These improvements went awry at the end of the quarter, however. With one week left in the pilot, the supplier's account salesperson believed he would not achieve his quarterly sales goal, even with the 10 percent sales revenue growth of the piloted product at the retailer. Doing what came naturally and a common practice, the salesperson offered the retail buyer a deal. Doing what comes naturally and a common practice, the buyer accepted the deal.

The result: The buyer purchased a four-week supply of future product, not for promotion, but for basic side counter inventory. A self-inflicted bullwhip resulted in a surprise order that caused everyone else to react and disrupted what had been a very smooth flow of predictable orders. The supplier had to work overtime over the weekend to get the orders assembled, which also included some expensive airfreight costs. The supplier also depleted product that was intended for its other retail customers.

The salesperson received a $5,000 quarterly bonus even though it cost his own company thousands of dollars in profits. No one could blame the salesperson, as he did what had always been acceptable — reach the sales revenue target no matter how it impacted profit. The retail buyer did what she had been trained to do — buy the product at the lowest cost possible.

There was a silver lining in this early collaboration failure. The implementation of the pilot included fairly rigorous documentation of the results, which was presented to the CEOs of both companies. Because the CPFR® pilot had been structured well, baseline performance metrics and measurements were taken at the start of the implementation and then recorded every week during the twelve-week pilot. Analysis was included as part of the performance measurement. In determining why the supplier did not achieve its sales revenue target, the source of the shortfall was not the retailer who partnered on the CPFR® pilot. The shortfall came from other retail customers.

When the CEOs were shown the actual cost of the deal offered by the supplier's salesperson to ensure meeting the supplier's sales revenue target, it resulted in a change in behavior from both the retailer as well as the supplier. On the supplier side, forecast accuracy was added to the individual salesperson's performance metric and bonus incentive. This provided a better balance than rewarding the attainment of a sales revenue target no matter the cost to company profits. Product profitability was also added as a team incentive for everyone including the salesperson. On the retailer side, forecast accuracy was also added to the buyers' individual performance metrics. The purpose was to help the placement of "surprise" or short-notice orders, which result in additional costs for inventory, labor handling, and inventory storage.

The lessons learned from early supply chain collaboration wins and failures are significant. In the case of the failures, the visibility of the cause and effect usually surfaces change management issues that need to be addressed. This should not be a surprise when implementing any type of process improvement, including CPFR®. Most companies have some type of poor business practices and behaviors that have been in place so long that people will say, "This is how we've always done it."

In today's highly competitive world, many companies cannot afford to operate as individual, disconnected business enterprises. Through both the successes and failures of early CPFR® efforts, it has been proven that a well-operating, integrated supply chain is a competitive advantage. The supply chain is no longer seen as just the cost of doing business; it is now seen as a competitive lever.

The companies that encountered some of the greatest failures in collaboration did not abandon the effort. They have become some of the greatest advocates and practitioners of collaboration. The next chapter, and indeed the rest of the book, provides a roadmap for the steps to take in implementing supply chain collaboration. This roadmap is based on the successes and failures of early collaboration efforts.

QUESTIONS

1. What are some of the benefits of actually executing a collaborative program versus observing other companies collaborating?
2. What three primary processes does a collaborative pilot help in identifying strengths and weaknesses?
3. What is considered the "lifeblood" of the supply chain?
4. What is considered a downfall in vendor managed inventory programs?

7

HOW TO IMPLEMENT SUPPLY CHAIN COLLABORATION

The most valuable investment in time and effort is in the early planning and development of a supply chain collaboration partnership. A partnership implies dependence on one another. A partnership implies that the partners have something to gain from the partnership. In evaluating the most successful collaboration efforts, they have the following in common in how they developed the collaboration partnerships (see Figure 31).

The first step (after determining that there is a desire to collaborate) is to develop a team with representatives from both business enterprises. All aspects of a business organization are typically impacted by supply chain collaboration. Therefore, it is crucial that the team is cross-functional in its representation (see Figure 32). This enables all functions that will be impacted to provide their insight as well as to have a voice in the development of the collaboration definition and design.

Figure 32 represents the typical functions in a retailer's organization as well as the manufacturer's organization. Supply chain collaboration works for all industries; feel free to use this chart as a template and apply your own functions to each of the circles.

The organizational functions closest to the center of the chart typically are more involved in the day-to-day supply chain collaboration functions. It is important to note, however, that all functions shown have some involvement in the collaborative effort as they all can impact the flow of product.

- Cross-functional teams from both enterprises are assigned
- Cross-functional teams include executive sponsors, senior directors, and process users as project team members
- Education sessions with team members from both enterprises are conducted to better understand each other's businesses and current planning and replenishment processes
- Workshop sessions with team members from both enterprises are conducted to define the business arrangement and to create a joint business plan
- The products that will be included in the supply chain collaboration effort are identified and agreed on
- Metrics and scorecards are agreed on
- A pilot program is defined and agreed on, including how the process will function and roles and responsibilities
- The pilot results are reviewed and presented to the executive sponsors to determine whether to continue to collaborate and how to improve the collaboration process

Figure 31.   Characteristics of Successful Collaboration Effort.

We have noted over the years how many functions within a company do not believe that they have an impact or play a role in the supply chain. The assignment of cross-functional team members will bring out this lack of understanding, usually immediately. This is good. It provides opportunity to develop an awareness of how almost all functions, in some way, cause the supply chain to operate either well or less well.

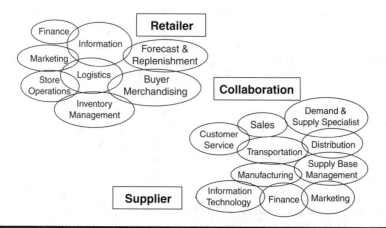

Figure 32.   Organizational Alignment. (©2004 Oliver Wight International.)

If functional representatives are not willing to participate in the team, this is your first warning signal that the supply chain collaboration effort may not succeed or will not yield the maximum benefits. If senior executives are unwilling to sponsor the effort, this is another warning signal. Without senior executive leadership and support, most collaborative efforts fail to develop a win/win benefit for both business enterprises.

It is a best practice for collaboration teams to have the following representation:

- Executive sponsors
- Senior directors from the functional groups
- Process users as project team members

Supply chain collaboration can be a transformational strategy for a company, so it is important to have executive sponsorship and top executive management support for the effort. Figures 33 and 34 describe the responsibilities of the executive team in developing and sustaining trading partner collaboration.

In addition to the executive committee, a senior operating team is needed to perform the responsibilities shown in Figure 35.

While the executive committee and senior operating team provide leadership and direction, the project team is responsible for executing the partnership. The project team's responsibilities are shown in Figure 36.

As indicated in the figures, it is important that each team member is educated on the supply chain collaboration principles and processes and has a good understanding of how the business enterprise and supply chain will benefit from

---

- Executives must be knowledgeable on what trading partner collaboration is and how it can benefit the entire company
- Executives must understand that transformational impact of adopting a trading partner collaboration program usually requires corporate change in the following areas:
    - Culture
    - Organizational
    - Performance metrics and incentives
    - Trust
    - Technology
- The CEO and COO must have a collaborative win/win relationship with the trading partner's CEO/COO

Figure 33.   Executive-Level Roles in Trading Partner Collaboration Strategy. (©2004 Oliver Wight International.)

- Vice presidents with the executive sponsor as champion
- All functional areas must be represented
- The executive committee must be educated on trading partner collaboration and how it works
- The executive committee must be committed to developing and sustaining partner relationships at the executive level
- The executive committee needs to support the process with priority and funding
- The executive committee serves as the transformational decision makers

Figure 34. Executive Sponsorship Committee. (©2004 Oliver Wight International.)

- Director-level responsibility
- Assign the resources to support the trading partnership program
- Operating team must be aligned with trading partner's operating team
- Balance "real-world" performance needs with trading partnership opportunities

Figure 35. Senior Operating Team. (©2004 Oliver Wight International.)

- Cross-functional team
- Members who have day-to-day supply chain responsibility are most involved and impacted
- Team is responsible for actual execution of trading partner collaboration program
- Team must be educated on the details of trading partner relationships and collaboration
- This team must be top individuals who have a strong commitment to the success of a trading partnership program
- Team members are willing to think out of the box
- Team members know the "as-is" state of the business well
- Team members know where supply chain performance can be improved through trading partnerships
- Team is aligned with trading partner's cross-functional team

Figure 36. Trading Partner Project Team. (©2004 Oliver Wight International.)

collaboration. In essence, those participating in the trading partner collaboration effort become advocates for the process and opportunists in developing collaborative methods for better serving customers and reducing waste and cost throughout the supply chain.

One of the best ways to launch a supply chain collaboration program is to start with a series of kickoff educational workshops. The most successful education approaches start with interactive workshops for the executive team that normally last a half day. In this executive session, the high-level concepts of trading partner collaboration are presented. The executives also explore and discuss how trading partner collaboration will benefit the enterprise.

The deliverables from this session should include a mission statement, broad guidelines for the senior operating team and project team, an endorsement of the collaborative program, and commitment to consider the program a high corporate priority. If the executives are unwilling to endorse the supply chain collaboration program, there is great risk in going forward. In our experience, a program achieves marginal results when executives are not committed to it. They will be unwilling to invest the company's time and resources in implementing the program, and they will not play the leadership role with the trading partners' executives that is needed to truly develop win/win relationships.

The senior operating team and project team need a deep and detailed understanding of trading partner collaboration. It is most effective when both teams participate in the education together. This joint session addresses in detail how the collaboration program will work, lessons learned from other collaboration programs, and the implementation steps. This education session typically lasts one or two days.

Both the executive workshop and the joint session for the senior operating team and project team should focus on the basics of supply chain collaboration. The following three basic components of supply chain collaboration should be addressed:

- Collaborative planning, including developing a front-end arrangement and joint business plan
- Collaborative forecasting, including the process for forecasting demand, communicating order schedules, and collaborating on exceptions
- Collaborative replenishment and order execution, including the process for order generation and delivery execution

Most education sessions will address the concepts shown in Figure 37.

Once the education sessions are completed, it is time to roll up the sleeves and get to work planning the collaboration effort. This usually involves a two- to four-day internal workshop in which the project team reviews the current

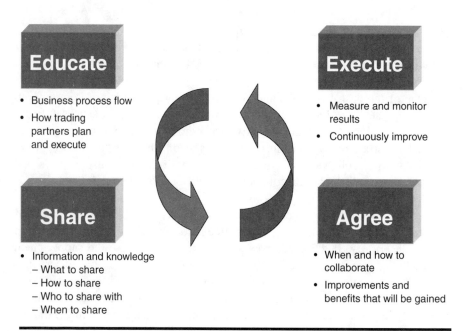

Figure 37. How Supply Chain Collaboration Works. (©2004 Oliver Wight International.)

internal processes and determines what is needed to develop collaborative processes. This planning session is, in our opinion, one of the most important steps of a successful collaboration program. The deliverable from this planning phase is a draft of a front-end arrangement and the creation of a joint business plan. It is important to understand how each process operates, how the processes flow, and the integration and interaction of functional areas. It also is necessary to understand the technology used to support the current planning and replenishment processes and how and when decisions and commitments are made.

Feel free to start with existing process flow charts and document any missing elements. When process flow charts do not exist, use butcher paper to document the process flow and decision points from one end of the supply chain to the other.

While documenting the process flow, it is important to discuss and document the time phase commitments that must be made to run the business, such as when manufacturing must commit to actually produce the product. It is also important to understand what information is needed and available to make those business decisions, such as a demand plan to drive the development of the production plan and schedule. The team also should discuss how supply chain collaboration can improve the current business process flows.

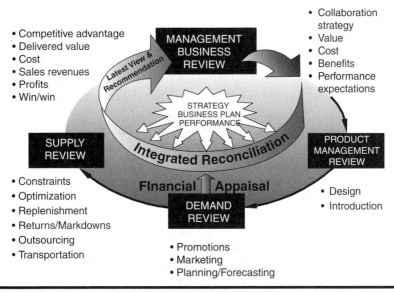

Figure 38.   Collaboration Opportunities. (©2004 Oliver Wight International.)

Once the "as-is" flow is defined, the next step is to define what the potential "to-be" process flow could look like. This also involves teaching each other the business by discussing improvement opportunities that a supply chain collaboration program can offer. This is very stimulating work that requires visionaries who can think out of the box. The discussion centers on what needs to change for our business process to improve and how both enterprises could benefit from collaboration.

There usually are many opportunities for collaboration, as shown in Figure 38. The discussion should identify what business process will be the first focus of collaboration.

Once the focus of the collaborative effort is agreed upon, the teams get down to defining such details as:

- What information should we share with each other?
- Who should receive the information?
- How should the information be shared?
- When should the information be communicated?
- How will the information be used?

In determining the above, time fences or decision points also need to be defined. These are the points in time when commitments or decisions must be made as part of the business process. It is at these points in time that action will be taken and, therefore, collaboration should have occurred to ensure the best decision for both enterprises. One example is reviewing the forecast exceptions and mutually agreeing on a single forecast of demand. It is important to understand these points of collaboration to ensure that the best collaboration efforts have taken place before it is too late and negative consequences occur. In identifying the points of collaboration, it is also necessary to define the roles, responsibilities, and accountability within both enterprises for ensuring that the collaboration occurs. This ensures common expectation and prevents misunderstandings from occurring.

Agreeing on the business arrangement between partners is vital. The front-end arrangement, as the VICS CPFR® organization has labeled it, is the instrument to capture the results of the project team kickoff and to document how the collaboration effort will work internally first and externally with a trading partner second. The front-end arrangement should document how the collaboration process will work, the goals and objectives, metrics, mission, and the roles and responsibilities. The VICS CPFR® organization has published a template of a front-end arrangement (see the Appendix) that is a useful guide for developing your own documentation. This template should be tailored to fit your particular company and trading partner(s) needs. It also is important to revisit the arrangement periodically and update it. The front-end arrangement should be considered a living document and should be modified based on new learning and new opportunities to add to the partnership.

Selecting the right partner is crucial. It is as important as selecting the right mate in marriage. We recommend selecting a trading partner that is important to your company and has the same desire as you to develop a win/win relationship. Let's be honest. Some business enterprises are just not very good collaboration partners, as will be discussed in the chapter on trading partner collaboration readiness later in this book.

In identifying candidates for a trading partner relationship, think of significance and think strategy. Draw candidates using the 80/20 rule — those 20 percent of trading partners that account for 80 percent of the financial business. Do not overlook strategic partners, however. Consider which partners strategically fit your company's future direction and how the two business enterprises might grow and prosper together.

As part of identifying business enterprises to partner with, you must also consider which products to include in the collaborative effort. Some products are better suited than others for collaboration. Figure 39 provides some basic guidelines for selecting products to include in the collaboration program.

- Use no more than ten products for a collaboration pilot
- Core image product — what your company is known for
  - Basic replenishment
  - Promotion
- Product that is strategic to you and your customer
  - Requires highest service level performance
- Product that is having supply chain problems
  - High out-of-stocks
  - Excessive inventory
  - Poor forecasting
  - Poor scorecard performance
- Highly seasonal
  - Product flow and forecasted demand
- Promotional
  - Poor forecast of demand

Figure 39. Guidelines for Selecting Products. (©2004 Oliver Wight International.)

An increasing number of companies keep scorecards on their suppliers' performance. Scorecards and metrics are needed for collaboration program performance as well. These scorecards focus on both partners' performance in the program.

One of the important lessons learned from the many successful supply chain collaboration programs is to keep the metrics and scorecards simple. Focus on the core measurements and do not overcomplicate the process.

The following are the core metrics that should be included in all scorecards:

- Forecast accuracy
- Sales revenue
- Inventory levels
- In-stock percentage
- Logistics costs
- Customer service levels

Documenting the number of emergencies, cost of the emergencies, and the reasons for the emergencies is also recommended. This helps to identify lapses in the partnering discipline and opportunities for improving the collaboration process as well as internal planning and execution processes.

In discussing and agreeing on metrics, it is important that the scorecard is balanced. By balanced we mean that it measures and reports both partners' performance and results. Also, it means that the metrics do not encourage counterproductive behaviors and actions. For example, one metric should be inventory levels. High inventory turns is desirable; running out of stock is not. Stockouts, of course, reduce sales revenue, which should be a performance metric as well.

In developing and executing performance metrics, both business enterprises should determine whether incentive programs are properly tuned to support the collaboration program. It is not unusual to need to rework incentives that reward the wrong effort or behavior. For example, all supply chain team members should be measured on forecast accuracy. Inaccurate demand forecasts result in higher inventory than needed and lost sales opportunities. It will become obvious that as forecast improves, so too will inventory levels and sales revenues.

Once the internal project team has completed the initial workshop and developed an internal front-end arrangement, the trading partner selected should be approached with a request to participate in a supply chain collaborative partnership pilot. In many cases, you may be the one who is approached first.

If the trading partner has already participated in other collaboration efforts, then it is good to go straight to scheduling a face-to-face team meeting between the two teams. If the trading partner has not participated in a collaborative program, most probably some education will be required and the trading partner should conduct its own internal workshop to map its process flows and develop its front-end arrangement and performance scorecard, as described above.

When the two project teams first meet, it is good to allow plenty of time to discuss how the collaboration effort can work, the business opportunities in collaborating, and the goals for the effort. This can take up to two days.

A good way to start the face-to-face session is to present an overview of the internally generated front-end arrangements and provide an overview of the business process flow charts that each partner has developed independently. This discussion is often called teaching each other the business. Project team members from both enterprises focus on collaborative opportunities. Discussion should center on:

- Where are the collaboration points?
- What information should we share with each other?
- Who should receive the information?
- How should the information be shared?
- When should the information be communicated?
- How will the information be used?

The outcome of this discussion will become input into a joint business plan. The joint business plan documents the focus of the collaborative effort, how the effort will be conducted, and the desired outcome and financial results. For example, some of the more common joint business plans focus on promotional strategies, marketing efforts, seasonal planning, new product introductions, new store growth, assortment planning, transportation planning, and financial planning.

The result of the face-to-face meeting should be a formally documented front-end arrangement and joint business plan. As you can see, both enterprises leverage the same type of collaborative planning processes by using similar workshops both internally and externally to create the final collaboration plan.

It should be noted that the degree of formality with regard to the front-end arrangement and joint business plan varies from company to company. Some companies will convert the front-end arrangement into a formal agreement, requiring executive signatures and in some cases with legal ramifications. Other companies use the documentation as a guideline or a process of mutual understanding, but leave room for what they may define as "real world" interruptions.

I cannot tell you what the best practice is other than you need to look at your company's culture and business philosophies on how official the documentation needs to be. My recommendation is that you and your trading partners follow the agreed-upon arrangement and joint business plan as closely as possible. Document the reasons for any deviations so that adjustments can be made and subsequently documented. Remember that the front-end arrangement and joint business plan should be considered "living" documents that are updated to reflect changes and improvements made to the collaboration program.

The majority of supply chain partnering efforts focus on forecasting demand. Thus, there is merit in reviewing how to implement demand collaboration programs.

The first step involves defining the hierarchical level to forecast, what products will be included in the collaboration program, and the type of forecasting that will be involved — sales forecasting, order forecasting, or both.

Determining the hierarchy level to forecast requires reviewing at what supply chain point the forecast will be consumed or used to execute the business processes. For example, in the retail store level, replenishment requires forecasting at the store level. In most supply chain collaboration programs, however, the collaborative relationship (and thus the forecasting) is at the distribution center level. That is to where product is most often shipped by the supplier. Even when the demand collaboration program focuses on the distribution center, there are times when it is advantageous to also focus at a lower level of detail, such as at the store level.

For many companies, an additional feedback loop on the demand plan comes from the manufacturer's internal sales and operations planning process. Through sales and operations planning, supply constraints and optimization opportunities are identified. These conditions result in recommendations that the supplier makes to the trading partner. Then both parties work together to reach consensus on their mutual forecasts of demand.

One good rule to follow with regard to the hierarchical level of the forecast is to collaborate at the lowest level that is practical. It is advantageous to get as close to the consumer or end user as possible. There is a saying: "If you mind your pennies, the dollars will manage themselves." This saying applies to getting close to the point of consumption. If a relatively accurate lower level, or detailed, forecast can be developed, then higher levels of aggregation of that forecast will be accurate as well, and the actual execution process will reflect better performance in the form of product availability and fewer stockouts. If the aggregated forecast is not accurate, then you will need to drill down to the lower levels of demand and determine the cause and effect.

The difference between sales forecasting and order forecasting needs to be well understood. Both are referred to differently in different industries. In drawing distinctions between the two, we utilize the retail and consumer goods industry terminology.

The sales forecast is typically defined as the forecast of demand consumption for product by the end user or consumer. In the case of a retailer, the sales forecast is known as a point-of-sale forecast; in other words, the product that is scanned at the cash register. In other industries, the sales forecast is the actual consumption of the product by the next link in the supply chain, often called the customer. In this case, the sales forecast could be warehouse withdrawals.

The sales forecast is one of the most important parts to a collaborative relationship as it enables focusing on the point of consumption. Much more is involved in sales forecasting than a statistically derived projection of demand consumption. Sales forecasting involves capturing and considering individual intelligence and knowledge on buyer preferences, demographics, and activities designed to influence buying behavior. It is within the sales forecasting process where partners collaborate on how planned promotions are expected to increase sales. Through the sales forecasting process, trading partners also evaluate and determine a product's true seasonality at the lowest levels in the supply chain. They also work together to understand and anticipate the impact of planning marketing advertising campaigns.

During our collaboration workshop, we will discuss with the trading partners where a sales forecast is produced, how it is produced, and where is it used to run the business. Our goal is to get to a "single forecast" that both trading partners can use to execute the business processes. Getting to a single forecast number can be done in two ways primarily:

1. Consensus: both trading partners provide sales forecasts, the forecasts are compared to each other, and the gaps are collaborated on to finally come up with an agreed single number.
2. One trading partner produces the sales forecast as a starting point and the collaboration is done on this forecast.

The sales forecasting process should be thoroughly discussed in the workshop session with the two trading partners. The partners should gain an understanding of how the sales forecast collaboration process should work. This involves discussing the strengths and weaknesses of each trading partner's processes and technology. Points of collaboration should be determined, including identifying which causal factors of demand will benefit from a collaborative approach. When causal factors of demand are well understood, adjustments can be made to a historical, statistically based forecast. New events, such as promotions, new item introductions, future store openings, and market intelligence, can then be factored into the statistically based forecast, resulting in a more accurate reflection of future demand.

The sales forecasting collaboration process should be addressed in the front-end arrangement. Roles and responsibilities of both trading partners in developing the sales forecast should also be agreed upon and documented in the front-end arrangement.

In defining the sales forecasting process, how forecast exceptions will be handled should also be addressed and agreed upon. There will always be exceptions, or errors, in any forecast. Rather than ignoring this probability, measures are needed for managing forecast errors. An added factor, especially in the retail industry, is the number of product items that are in stores. This number can exceed fifty thousand SKUs per store. With that many product items to manage, it is impossible to review every SKU item by item when developing the sales forecast. As a result, an exception management method is needed.

The exception management approach involves allowing the software system to identify when individual product items exceed preset tolerances. The tolerances are set for conditions or events that trading partners desire to manage. When the tolerances are exceeded, the software issues an alert, which is communicated to the appropriate person to review and respond to. Examples of conditions or events that typically are included in exception management are:

- Forecast error greater than X percent
- Promotional lift greater than XX percent

- Differences between the two trading partners' forecasts of XX percent
- Performance metrics below agreed-upon tolerances

In addition to defining exceptions to monitor, time fences also should be agreed upon. In actuality, time fences are decision points. Time fences usually demark time frames where there is greater or lesser risk in changing the forecast. Thus, there is greater or lesser flexibility for accommodating changes in demand. I like to define these time periods as follows:

- **Liquid**: This is the longer range time period where change demand forecasts will have little impact on trading partners. The demand information is used to help determine needed future capability. The demand information in this time zone frequently is considered as guidance, rather than a commitment.
- **Slushy**: This is a medium-range time period in which there is more certainty, or confidence, about future demand. Frequently, the volume may be correct in the medium-range time zone, but the timing of the demand will be less certain. There needs to be some flexibility to change the demand plan within this zone.
- **Frozen**: This is a shorter range time period when there is the least flexibility to change. Production has already begun or shipments to the retailer are already on their way. That is why this zone is frequently considered "frozen." In actuality, sometimes changes in demand can be accommodated in this time period; however, it is almost always at a higher cost.

Trading partners should agree on the time fences and the process for managing change within each time period. These decisions should be documented in the front-end arrangement. The definition of time zones frequently includes exception management tolerances, such as XX percent over the previously communicated sales forecast. With regard to managing changes in demand within the "frozen" time zone, the rule of thumb is to define one partner that will make the final decision as to whether or not to accept the change. The partner determined to be the final decision maker should be the partner that incurs the most risk and cost in making the change.

Order forecasting involves different rules, policies, and management techniques than sales forecasting. For those familiar with distribution resource planning, the order forecast used in supply chain collaboration is similar to a time series replenishment-based forecast of the actual purchase orders.

Order forecast collaboration normally involves defining order policy file rules and optimization opportunities. Some examples are:

- Vendor minimums
- Lead times
- Safety stock settings
- Minimum and maximum shelf capacities
- Order points
- Customer service levels
- Pack sizes
- Pallet configurations
- Truck loading

Once agreement is reached on the order policy file settings, order forecasts can be created using the "best fit" forecasting algorithms within the technology, using the sales forecast as the demand input.

After the order forecast is generated, the manufacturer uses it as input into its demand planning and sales and operations planning processes to determine whether the product can actually be produced. (Sales and operations planning will be covered in detail later in the book.) The order forecast will also be reviewed to identify optimization opportunities that will yield reduced cost of goods sold, such as optimizing transportation and manufacturing.

Before embarking on full-scale collaboration on sales forecasting, order forecasting, or other collaboration programs, it is wise to pilot the collaboration process first. Most collaboration pilots yield unexpected lessons that cannot be learned just from studying or "white boarding" a process.

The question is: How long should the pilots run before being expanded to include more products? The duration of the pilot should consider product life cycle and seasonality. For example, if you have a product that is seasonal, you will want to conduct the pilot through the planning cycles for the season as well as the season itself. For basic replenishment products, you would want the pilot to last long enough to see the impact on the actual manufacturing cycle. For promotional products, the pilot should include the planning and actual execution of the promotion, culminating in the buying of the promoted product by consumers or end users.

Some products, such as apparel, have longer lead times than, say, ketchup. For longer lead time products, the collaboration pilot should last a complete cycle, from conception to commercialization. This can be as long as a year or more.

The future time zones and level of detailed information that are communicated for the pilot should also be considered and defined. In most retail and consumer goods pilots, the future time zone involved is typically weekly "buckets" for twelve weeks and monthly "buckets" for six months. In the apparel industry, weekly "buckets" are considered closer to the season, and monthly or even quarterly "buckets" are used for up to eighteen months in the future.

In determining the duration of your collaboration pilot, here is some advice:

- Make sure the pilot test lasts long enough to test the consumption of the forecast.
- Pilot just long enough to gain lessons learned and then decide improvements and changes to be made.

Once all the planning and preparation work has been completed for a collaboration program, it is time to actually execute the pilot according to the front-end arrangement and joint business plans that have been created. The front-end arrangement and business plans have defined exactly how the collaboration effort is going to work, including the generation of demand forecasts, roles and responsibilities, system exceptions that trigger alerts, and the generation of the purchase order. Now executing the pilot according to the plan is nothing more than doing what was promised and agreed to do.

During the pilot, the team members from both partners will perform the necessary reviews, collaborate internally and externally according to the agreements, and make any adjustments that are necessary to improve performance. It is important to remember that the supply chain collaboration effort is a journey and you will learn from actually doing it. The agreements can be adjusted as the teams find the need to adjust. It also is extremely important for the leaders of the trading partner project to keep a running journal of how the pilot is progressing, performance, and the lessons learned.

So how much time should you expect to be expended on a pilot? Figures 40 and 41 show the typical time required for retailers and manufacturers. The main point is that experience has shown that this is not labor intensive. In fact, many retailers and manufacturers alike report that they spend less time than prior to collaboration on "fire fighting" caused by stockouts and managing changes in demand. They spend more qualitative time focused on becoming more customer centric and growing their brands and categories.

The figures are examples of how much time it typically takes to perform a collaborative pilot for a retailer as well as a manufacturer. Many companies that have gone through pilots and are now beyond the pilot stage have stated that no additional people needed to be added as emergencies were reduced to the point that the collaboration was just part of the normal routine.

— **One hour per day average**
  • Forecast and Replenishment Analyst
— **One hour per week average**
  • Buyer
  • Inventory Management
— **As-needed basis**
  • Information Technology
  • Logistics
— **Monthly meeting**
  – Project Team

Figure 40. Retailer Project Team Time Commitments. (©2004 Oliver Wight International.)

Finally, after the pilot is complete, both trading partners should document and share the following with one another and their respective senior management teams:

■ What were the lessons learned?
■ What were the benefits?
■ What were the costs?
■ What technology is needed to enable expanding collaboration to other products with this partner and to other trading partners?

— **One hour per day average**
  • Customer Service
  • Demand and Supply Specialist
— **One hour per week average**
  • Sales
— **As-needed basis**
  • Information Technology
  • Transportation
  • Distribution
— **Monthly meeting**
  • Project Team

Figure 41. Manufacturer Project Team Time Commitments. (©2004 Oliver Wight International.)

- What is your recommendation for going forward with supply chain collaboration?
- How does supply chain collaboration fit with your company's current strategic plans?
- How does supply chain collaboration fit with your company's future strategies and goals?

QUESTIONS

1. What are the three collaborative teams?
2. What functional areas are represented on each team?
3. Which functions are usually most impacted by a supply chain collaboration program?
4. What are the three basic components to a supply chain collaboration program?
5. Where and how do you document the collaboration agreement?
6. How does "teaching each other the business" work?
7. What were the core metrics used for measuring the performance levels of collaboration?
8. What are collaboration points?
9. How long should a collaborative pilot last?
10. What are some of the factors in an order policy file?
11. What is the difference between a sales forecast and an order forecast?
12. What are the three time fences or periods to a forecast?

TECHNOLOGY OVERVIEW

Supply chain collaboration technology is a critical part in the actual execution of the collaborated decisions that have been made. Many companies have failed in the area of having the proper technology infrastructures and have minimized some of the potential benefits that a good technology architecture can offer. Although we have seen success with what we may define as "manual collaboration" efforts, the truth to the matter is that for us to take collaboration to scale as well as to much lower levels of detail, technology is necessary.

Supply chain collaboration technology requires certain components. Below are some examples of the technology that may be required for your collaborative efforts.

- Forecasting
  - □ Statistical-based forecasting engines for sales and order forecasting
  - □ Causal-based forecasting contributions
- Collaboration
  - □ Collaboration software that can compare two or more forecasts to each other to derive a single consensus-based forecast number
  - □ Allows for tolerances and alerts to be established as defined by the collaborative agreements and joint business plans
  - □ Provides for the adjustments to forecasts according to the collaborative agreements
  - □ Provides text-based communication linkage for trading partner collaboration to document reasons for forecast changes or adjustments
  - □ Generates the agreed to single forecast number

- Business-to-business (B2B) communication or linkage
  - ☐ Electronic data interchange (EDI)
    - 830 — forecasts
    - 852 — sales actuals and inventory levels
  - ☐ Extended machine language (XML)
    - Internet-based B2B communication
    - VICS CPFR® standard-based models
- Replenishment
  - ☐ Automated replenishment systems used at the various levels of product consumption typically driven by forecasted days of supply and reorder point calculations as well as distribution resource planning (DRP)–based algorithms
- Data warehouses
  - ☐ Informational stores of data to be used for trading partner information sharing, statistical forecasting, planning, data mining, as well as replenishment
- Enterprise resource planning (ERP)
  - ☐ Totally integrated foundational system architectures that provide for closed-loop processing and execution; typically range from financial applications through manufacturing
- Advance planning and scheduling (APS)
  - ☐ Demand planning forecasting
  - ☐ "What if" simulations
  - ☐ Optimization for manufacturing planning and scheduling
- Planning technology
  - ☐ Transportation
  - ☐ Merchandising and assortments
  - ☐ Promotional
  - ☐ Marketing
  - ☐ Events

The above list of technology is primarily a core list of applications, but it is not intended to be all-inclusive. You will have to access your own technology infrastructure and develop a plan on what will work best for you and your collaborative partnerships. The important fact to embrace is to execute the business decisions that are collaborated and agreed to. If we fail to execute, then we will fail to reap the benefits of the collaboration. Allowing our technology systems to go on an "autopilot" mode and have collaboration only performed on the exceptions is key for the most successful supply chain programs.

COLLABORATION SOFTWARE

Because this book is on supply chain collaboration, we can focus on the technology that has been recently developed to support trading partner collaboration. In 1997, the VICS CPFR® Working Group established a technology team to develop the technology standards and guidelines for collaboration. The technology standards developed were first published in 1998 and continue to be updated and revised today; you can review the technology standards at www.cpfr.org. We have also seen collaboration technology guidelines established by other industries, such as the Hi Tech's RosettaNet as well as the Supply Chain Council's SCOR model.

The collaboration standards as established by the VICS CPFR® Working Group subcommittee address the issues of:

- Data modeling
  - ☐ File layouts
- Text messaging
  - ☐ Definitions to information messaging including e-mail text
- Interoperability
  - ☐ B2B linkage guidelines so systems can communicate to each other
- Security
  - ☐ Data and text protection

The Uniform Code Council (UCC) has been extremely helpful in defining the standards for collaborative technology for the VICS CPFR® technology.

Collaboration technology has become the central portal to the trading partner collaborative effort. It is here where forecasts are shared between trading partners and the actual collaboration takes place. Collaboration software can be configured for the tolerances and alerts to function and provide the action messages to be sent to the responsible person on a daily basis if needed. The software provides for "exception management" collaboration so the end users are not buried in too much detail.

In addition, "forecast warning" signals can be defined in collaboration technology to help prevent potential surprises or disasters. For example, if a forecast for a certain week changes beyond a predefined percentage from the previous week's forecast run, an alert or warning message can be generated to a specific user mailbox for the individual to review for a potential correction or acknowledgment that it is okay.

Collaboration technology also allows for drill-down capabilities so the exceptions can be researched more easily. For example, if the two trading partners are collaborating at a distribution center level, they can go below the distribution center level to the store level to see what may be causing the issues.

Collaboration technology is also valuable to provide each trading partner with notifications of events, such as for promotions or holiday planning. The technology also provides for e-mail-type text messaging to be communicated that is attached to the points of collaboration that will provide the necessary information on why a trading partner has performed the adjustments.

The industry-leading technology companies have helped develop the VICS CPFR® technology guideline standards in a spirit of cooperation and collaboration that is seldom witnessed and has made the development of their own unique solutions possible while still supporting the need for system interoperability. Because these free, public domain, industry technology standards are available, some companies have elected to develop their own "in-house" collaborative solutions.

EXCHANGES

Exchanges have emerged to further support supply chain collaboration and the sharing of trading partner data. These exchanges are used to share information between trading partners, such as forecasts, data on products such as actual sales history, point of sale (POS), inventory positions, metrics and scorecards, to the actual collaboration software. The trading partners are only given access to their own products.

The exchanges are in three primary forms:

- Private
  - Hosted by one of the trading partners on its server, behind its firewall
  - Access provided to trading partner through an intranet, extranet, or the Internet
  - Proprietary solution, often developed in-house
  - Preferred by some companies as a more secured environment for data protection
- Public
  - A private company that provides an exchange service for a fee
  - Considered to have the advantage of bringing multiple trading partners into the same exchange for easier critical mass application and collaboration consistency
  - Collaboration technology provided by one proven technology company

- □ Provides for a fast and low cost of entry into collaboration without the significant investment typically found with a private exchange
- □ Advertises data security and integrity are maintained
- ■ Hosted
  - □ Technology companies that offer collaboration software will host the collaboration effort on their own server for a fee
  - □ Advantage is easier integration of collaborative decisions into execution systems such as replenishment and manufacturing; no interfaces are needed
  - □ Considered a quick start for trading partners to begin collaborative pilots at a relatively inexpensive cost

EXAMPLES OF COLLABORATION TECHNOLOGY

To help further explain the collaboration technology, we have asked some of the leading collaborative technology solution providers to briefly highlight their approach to supply chain collaboration technology and the features and functions that they provide. We also asked them to provide screen shots of some of their solutions. We want to point out that we do not necessarily endorse the technology solutions below, but we do consider them good solutions that demonstrate how collaboration software can and does function. We also want to point out that there is also other good collaboration technology on the market. In addition, you can consider developing your own collaboration technology solutions in-house.

THE POWER OF AN EXECUTABLE SINGLE FORECAST*

Fred Baumann
Vice-President, Collaborative Solutions
The JDA Software Group

Introduction

The Collaborative Planning, Forecasting, and Replenishment (CPFR®) process has been heralded as one of the most promising business processes to eliminate waste and drive revenue for trading partners within the supply chain. Partners have successfully implemented demand-based CPFR® and have collected on the benefits. It is time to take CPFR® through to its true and complete vision. For this to occur, trading partners must accept a degree of risk and question the status quo of traditional business practices. Order forecast collaboration and commitment processing are the golden keys to the value chain vault. These keys are readily available for the brave few willing to break through to a higher order business process.

The vision of CPFR® is built on the foundation of a conceptual framework where trading partners contribute their unique insights and competencies to formulate a shared forecast of demand. An agreed-upon forecast of demand that includes joint commitment can minimize demand chain uncertainty and enable trading partners to better meet the needs of the ultimate consumer with less working capital. Lower inventory requirements to satisfy consumer demand has been an explicit goal for buyers and suppliers working within the CPFR® framework. While the realized benefits have been substantial, participants and prospects to the process are pondering many questions:

- Does the creation of a single forecast of demand between trading partners in and of itself provide the promise of lower inventory and greater sales?
- How do you ensure that there is an orderly progression from sales and order forecasting to order execution and delivery?
- What commitment processes should be included in the program in order to ensure that trading partners are vested to share risk and reward?

While the promise of CPFR® has been demonstrated and backed up by documented case studies, the industry adoption rate has been slow considering the process guidelines were published over seven years ago.

The framers of the CPFR® process model adopted three guiding principles that would guide the development of the business process model and deployment of the process in the marketplace. The guiding principles are:

1. A trading partner framework
2. A single shared forecast of demand
3. Joint commitment to the shared forecast through risk sharing and the removal of supply chain constraints

Much of the focus in the market has been placed on the first two guiding principles, with little progression exhibited on the last. To attain the true vision of CPFR® and move to the next level of benefits, participants must formulate a plan to execute against all guiding principles established within the CPFR® business model. Partners must take the proper steps to make the single forecast more accurate, more actionable, and easier to integrate into order execution.

This paper will highlight different approaches to these goals and provide suggestions for action.

The Trading Partner Framework: Guiding Principle #1

Suppliers and customers have unique insights and levels of experience that can be leveraged to optimize the strength of the supply chain. Each of these partners has particular information and insights into future events and activities that influence demand. These strengths will largely contribute to the successes of each partner in the collaboration. This knowledge ensures that forecasts are accurate and that service level targets can be attained with the optimum inventory investment.

The strength of the trading partner framework largely determines the degree of success of the entire process. The trading partner framework is the foundation on which the other principles rest. Much of the framework is formalized in the first step of the CPFR® process model: the development of the collaborative arrangement. During this step, the trading partners formalize the goals and objectives of their partnership, define the resources and systems required to execute the process, determine the level of information sharing, define exception and resolution processes, and determine the frequency by which their agreement is reviewed and published. The arrangement should clearly define the commitment processing that will take place between the partners as their processes become mature and formalized.

The Single Shared Forecast of Demand: Guiding Principle #2

The second guiding principle has received a great deal of focus from trading partners executing the process. Getting to the second principle assumes that a trading partner framework is in place to leverage the knowledge and competencies of both trading partners involved in the process.

Managing to a single demand forecast can ensure that trading partners are empowered to meet the needs of their respective customer. Working from the "same number" permits suppliers and buyers to lower safety stock requirements and reduce potential lost sales because the forecast is built on shared knowledge of demand. There is general agreement in the market that a single shared forecast of demand that leverages the knowledge of both trading partners is superior to forecasting in isolation. There are, however, different approaches to creating the single collaborative demand forecast:

- **Dual Forecast Approach** — The dual forecast approach starts with each trading partner generating a forecast independently of the other.

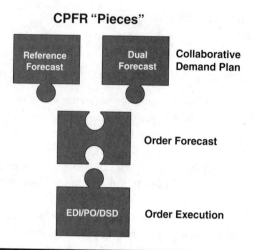

Figure 1.

The forecasts are then fed to a middleware engine that highlights where the forecasts differ based on predefined exception criteria established by the partners. The trading partners then collaborate on why the forecasts differ and come to resolution on a single number.

- **Reference Forecast Approach** — Trading partners begin with a reference forecast generated by one of the trading partner's systems. Each trading partner has visibility and execution rights to apply its independent knowledge to the forecast and make updates. Forecast exceptions enable trading partners to collaborate on the inputs of the forecast to come to resolution on a single shared forecast.

Creating a collaborative demand plan is only one of three main activities that occur in the CPFR® process. After the collaborative forecast is generated, either through a dual forecast model or a reference forecast model, it is necessary to transition the forecast into a replenishment plan for order generation (Figure 1). For trading partners that desire to move to the third guiding principle of CPFR®, there has to be a procurement methodology that balances the retail replenishment plan with available supply and capacity from the supplier.

Joint Commitment to the Shared Forecast: Guiding Principle #3

According to the third CPFR® guiding principle, partners commit to a shared forecast through mutual risk taking and the removal of supply process constraints. Committing to a customer-focused demand strategy based on real knowledge of each step in the trading process greatly reduces the uncertainty associated with sales and order forecasting. Adopting a single shared forecast of demand, suppliers can shift from a "build to stock" to "build to order" methodology that can greatly reduce the dependency on buffer inventory. Restraints such as fixed retail order cycles or inconsistent delivery and fill rates from suppliers can be greatly reduced.

Does the creation of a single forecast of demand between trading partners in and of itself provide the promise of lower inventory and greater sales? The exercise of creating a single shared demand forecast has been beneficial to most partners that have participated. Some of the greatest benefits of this exercise have come from the discovery of promotional events that would have caused much greater strains on the supply chain had they not been communicated. Seasonal trends and product-specific regionality can also be more accurately discovered through the collaborative forecasting process, adding greater sales and inventory velocity as well as operational cost improvements by incorporating this new knowledge in production planning and product deployment. The greatest benefits highlighted to date have been on the top-line sales side of the business. Trading partners are able to position the right products to the end consumer when they are looking to buy.

Many CPFR® trading partners will admit that they are still missing critical sales opportunities even when the shared forecast between the trading partners is accurate. Additionally, many of the partners will attest to the fact that while sales have improved due to the process, inventories required to meet the consumer demand are still higher than expected or desired. How can this be possible within the nirvana of a collaborative partnership? There are two primary drivers to this problem.

Driver 1: Often, There Is Not a Smooth Transition from the Sales Forecast to the Order Forecast to Final Order Execution and Delivery

The sales forecast represents projected sales from the store shelf to the consumer or, in some environments, the forecast of demand from the customer distribution centers to the store network. The order forecast represents what the customer is going to order from the supplier to meet the needs established in the sales forecast. Unfortunately, some trading partners have created separate, disconnected processes for developing the sales and order forecast. It is important to understand that the sales forecast and order forecast are inextricably linked. Thus, when a change occurs in the sales forecast, there should be a dynamic synchronization process that automatically adjusts the order forecast. The two forecasting processes cannot be approached independently.

To address this issue, it is important to understand the complexity involved with accurately providing an order forecast beyond one lead time with a required level of accuracy. Suppliers are typically very interested in the order forecast because it answers the question, *"What is my customer going to order and when?"* Having input and insight into the demand stream is very valuable, but in isolation does not provide enough information to assist in the commitment processing of production capacity and finished goods inventory planning.

Variables that must be considered for accurate sales forecast to order forecast translation include:

- On-hand and on-order inventory positions of the customer
- Order cycle/order frequency policies
- Changes to inventory policy (safety stock requirements — service level, weeks of supply)
- Shipping requirements (item min and max, order min and max)
- Lead time
- Unit translation (order/pack multiples)

Driver 2: There Is Limited Commitment Processing That Occurs Between Trading Partners to Ensure That Risks and Rewards Can Be Shared in an Automated Fashion

After trading partners agree on the single shared order forecast, there has to be a level of commitment that is given by both trading partners to achieve the vision of the third guiding principle of CPFR®. If manufacturers are going to move to "build to order" processing or significantly reduce safety stocks, there has to be a confidence level that the buyer is going to provide purchasing commitments beyond a typical lead time. The commitments should have a stated level of tolerance that can be decreased as the orders approach delivery. By contrast, in order for buyers to lower safety stocks and attain higher fill rates, they need commitments of supply from their respective suppliers and visibility to manufacturing constraints to meet consumer requirements efficiently. The ability to overcome this hurdle hinges on a level of confidence embedded in the order forecast. A trading partner's willingness to commit to an order forecast is directly correlated to the accuracy the order forecast has delivered over time.

A strong possibility exists that there are cultural barriers that have inhibited the adoption of commitment processing. Both trading partners have to take on a certain degree of risk to get to this level of a CPFR® relationship. Customers that provide a level of commitment to order beyond historical lead-time parameters should receive a level of commitment to supply beyond historical levels from suppliers. In order to reap the full rewards of collaboration, this step must be taken.

The table below displays a graphical view of how an order forecast might be displayed after the previously mentioned order adjustments are taken into account. Each column represents an order forecast that will eventually become an order. As time progresses, the columns will move to the left until the orders become live and tendered for shipment. It is important to note that if the order forecasting process is going to translate to order generation automatically, the entire vendor line must be taken into account. It does not make sense to execute a subset of items for this process within the vendor line unless that subset is tendered as a separate order.

Example: Projected Receipt Quantities and Dates

Item Number	Item Description	100% Committed		30	70% Committed				60
		5-Jan	18-Jan		1-Feb	12-Feb	5-Mar	21-Mar	
123456	SKU 1	120	543		345	380	434	6243	
123457	SKU 2	2321	345		3333	578	66	444	
123458	SKU 3	234	753		154	524	643	434	
123459	SKU 4	212	345		245	623	453	434	
123460	SKU 5	465	2345		667	35	4534	45	
123461	SKU 6	453	454		436	44	345	6443	
123462	SKU 7	753	345		643	234	543	455	
123463	SKU 8	545	754		345	553	453	643	

Commitment should be another "C" referenced in CPFR®. Commitment to the shared order forecast is perhaps the most important guiding principle of a CPFR® trading relationship. Unfortunately, there is not an additional letter in CPFR® to remind business leaders that the third guiding principle is perhaps the most important. Commitment provides a tangible demonstration that both trading partners will drive order execution based on the collaborative sales forecasting processes executed earlier in the relationship.

Figure 2 introduces the notion of "time-fencing" an order forecast after it has been calculated. A time fence, represented by the vertical solid lines, represents a point in time where the order forecast changes its degree of commitment by the collaborative trading partners.

From the customer's perspective, commitment is demonstrated by a willingness to purchase against the forecast. From a supplier's perspective, commitment means they will produce, deploy, and ship against the forecast. The example above shows that two time fences have been established as part of the relationship. The first time fence is sixty days out into the future. When order

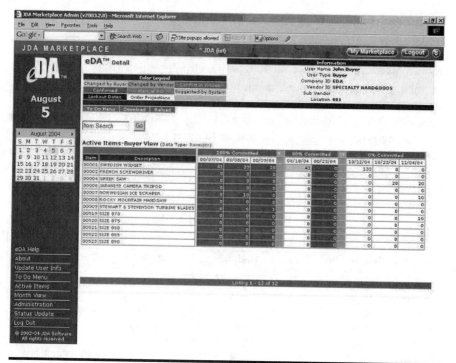

Figure 2.

forecasts pass this first fence, they are 70 percent committed or, conversely, the order quantities can vary by ±30 percent between thirty and sixty days. The second time fence is thirty days out into the future. When the order forecasts pass the thirty-day time fence, they become 100 percent committed. In essence, a purchase order is created with the quantities listed in the column that passes over the time fence.

This type of relationship is occurring today in a customer production environments using JDA Software. The product is named The Electronic Dynamic Agreement (eDA).

With commitment processing, you should walk before you run. The VICS CPFR® Voluntary Guidelines published in 1998 discuss the notion of a single time fence where the order forecast becomes a live order at a single point in time. In practice, it is likely that trading partners will establish multiple time fences with increasing levels of commitment as the order delivery date approaches. Suppliers have to make production decisions (how much) before they have to make distribution decisions (where to send it). Volume commitments might be made at the early time, with inventory deployment decision postponed until later. The result is that the buyer and the supplier can collaborate about decisions that have specific types of parameters at different times. These decisions drive specific cost implications that should produce benefits. Understanding those benefits should be the foundation for risk sharing. Trading partners can take measured steps to ensure that they feel comfortable and can meet the commitment parameters established in their collaborative arrangement.

For example, in the beginning of a collaborative relationship, the first time fence can be established at the traditional order lead time that was used to generate orders prior to the collaborative engagement. Order forecasts beyond the first time fence can be used for planning purposes only, with no implied commitment level. As the collaborative relationship matures and the partners feel more confident of the order forecasts that are being generated, additional time fences can be added with varying levels of commitment. This progression will be made easier if order forecasting accuracy measures are made available. Suppliers will obviously prefer that the commitment levels be as far in the future as possible with low tolerance for change. Customers will likely prefer shorter commitment windows and wider tolerance ranges. Suppliers may choose to provide incentives to their customers to provide longer commitment windows through menu-based pricing and terms options. The consumers will be the ultimate benefactor of commitment processing because the work of the collaborative forecasting will translate to executable product orders that provide stock availability when they are ready to buy.

Summary

CPFR® has and will continue to drive benefits for trading partners executing the process. Higher sales, reduced working capital, and healthier trading relationships are available for those that invest in and implement collaborative supply chain management. For trading partners that are contemplating starting a CPFR® program or are currently engaged in CPFR®, we offer the following advice:

- Consider leveraging the reference forecast approach for generating a single shared forecast of demand in cases where it makes sense with your trading partners.
- Move beyond demand forecast collaboration to order forecast collaboration.
- Ensure that your collaborative forecasting initiative impacts the ultimate replenishment order being generated.
- Take the third guiding principle of CPFR® to heart and begin to formulate plans to execute commitment processing with your trading partners.

Adopt an open attitude when starting new CPFR® initiatives with your trading partners. Experiment, learn, and benchmark against different ideas and methodologies. Best practices are likely to be adopted by incorporating a variety of processes.

ELECTRONIC DYNAMIC AGREEMENT™: THE FIRST SOLUTION TO GENERATE ORDER FORECASTS USING ACTUAL ORDER CREATION LOGIC WITH LINKED COMMITMENT PROCESSING*

Inside Scenario — What will your trading partners order and when? This may be one of the most fundamental yet complex supply chain questions to plague trading partners. Suppliers need accurate order projections to manufacture, pick, and ship goods more economically. Retailers want this addressed to improve first-time fill rates, on-time deliveries, and service levels. Both sides want to increase sales, product availability, and cash flow, while decreasing buffer inventory and logistical expenses. While partners can share point-of-sale (POS) information and sales forecasts, this information does not translate into a spot-on order forecast. What trading partners really need is improved long-term order visibility.

Electronic Dynamic Agreement (eDA): Answering What a Trading Partner Will Order and When

Retailers and suppliers can now rely on JDA's Electronic Dynamic Agreement™ (eDA™), an accurate and stable solution for their order forecasting and execution needs. Part of the Portfolio Collaborative Solutions™ suite, eDA is the first software to generate a retailer's order forecast dynamically for a supplier beyond the standard single-order lead time using order creation logic and commitment processing. By leveraging downstream demand with concrete order logistics translation variables, eDA can provide visibility as much as one year into the future.

Rather than relying solely on the sharing of sales forecasts and POS information, trading partners can take advantage of eDA's predictive algorithms that translate demand projections into order projections. Its projection logic smooths the impact of demand shifts and even offers an intuitive conflict resolution process.

Proven to Support VICS CPFR® Business Model

To prove eDA's sophisticated capabilities, JDA teamed with Ace Hardware, a past winner of the Best in VICS CPFR® Implementation and pioneer in advancing collaborative processes. Ace helped to drive eDA's design and test its functionality with a supplier. As a result, we can confidently state that eDA fully supports the execution of steps six to nine of the VICS CPFR® business model:

- Create order forecasts
- Identify order forecast exceptions
- Collaborate on exception items
- Generate orders

Remove Uncertainty from Translation Variables

The industry's need for the innovation that eDA delivers is due to a number of translation variables that have hampered the ability to create a sound order forecast. These evolving factors include:

- On-hand and on-order inventory positions of the customer
- The item economics or order cycle/order frequency policies
- Inventory policy changes (safety stock requirements — service level, weeks of supply)
- Shipping requirements (item min and max, order min and max)
- Lead time between when retailer needs to order and receive
- Item multiples or unit translation (order/pack multiples)

eDA automatically takes into consideration all of these variables along with sales forecasts, promotional activities, and deal buy opportunities to produce a reliable, stable order forecast that partners can share over the Internet.

Improve Order Visibility to Boost First-Time Fill Rates, Service Levels

By gaining critical visibility to customer orders beyond historical lead times, suppliers can more efficiently build orders available for delivery as scheduled. In fact, suppliers should even be able to reduce total cycle times.

Plus, suppliers will have the information that they need to completely fill orders. If there are any constraints that will slow down delivery of a complete order, eDA alerts can be created. Trading partners can then adjust their promotional or causal plans while there is still time to make execution decisions. As a result, retailers and wholesalers will gain better first-time fill rates to optimize profitability, service levels, and consumer satisfaction.

Optimize Production Planning to Drive Down Supply Chain Costs

Beyond planning for finished goods, eDA can help manufacturers further up the supply chain by integrating with advanced planning and scheduling (APS) systems or materials resource planning (MRP) systems. This will enable a manufacturer to reduce supply chain costs by making more informed decisions on how much and when to order raw material from its suppliers.

By leveraging the information from eDA, manufacturers can now make more informed decisions on their production and deployment strategies to drive down operational costs and inventory holding costs. These savings can either be passed down the supply chain to increasingly price-sensitive consumers or applied to the bottom line.

JDA Portfolio Collaborative Solutions™: Building a Stronger Supply Chain

What makes eDA such a compelling solution is that it is part of a unique and powerful suite: Portfolio Collaborative Solutions™. With more trading pairs than any other public retail exchange depending on Portfolio Collaborative Solutions to support over $3 billion in trading volume, we commit significant resources to ensure the most advanced functionality and business processes. Our methodology is based on defined practices and agreements so both sides understand their roles, responsibilities, and shared goals. And both sides achieve optimal results.

By working from the same page, buyers and suppliers can leverage their unique competencies and maximize efficiencies while minimizing uncertainty and improve stock availability while lowering inventory investments. Collaboration is a win-win for all involved.

In addition to eDA, you can choose from the following integrated applications to build your winning supply chain:

- **JDAMarketplace.com** — Allows trading partners to navigate easily and securely to collaborative solutions and partners via the Internet. The JDAMarketplace portal also provides educational insights and recent news for those interested in the collaborative space.
- **Marketplace Replenish** — Enables retailers and suppliers to realize supply efficiencies by jointly executing full-scale CPFR® programs

involving collaborative demand forecasting, exception management, and order generation securely over the Internet. Marketplace Replenish complements eDA by supporting steps three to five and nine of the VICS CPFR® business model.

eDA: Proven Functionality for Order Forecasting and Execution

- Dynamically generates accurate order projections based on collaborative demand forecasts
- Enables partners to share order forecasts over the Internet via JDAMarketplace.com or export the order forecasts for use in other applications
- Allows the supplier to confirm product availability linked to order projections easily
- Allows wholesalers and suppliers to commit to order forecasts beyond a regular order lead time
- Seamlessly generates orders from order forecasts based on trading partners' defined time periods
- Supports time fences and commitment percentage rules, plus creates exceptions based on commitment percentages and user changes
- Translates demand projections into vendor order projections with advanced algorithms

Problem: Inventory Availability

With Shrinking Customer Lead Time

(Supplier Supply Chain Process: Longer than Customer Lead time)

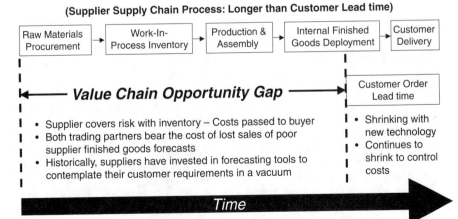

- Smooths the impact of demand shifts with sophisticated projection logic
- Supports ease of use with GUI front end and an intuitive conflict resolution process
- Allows for aggregation of order forecasts across locations
- Enables multiple alerts to align demand with supply
  - ☐ Constraints on supply from a quantity or timing perspective
  - ☐ Requests for additional supply, changes in timing, or both
  - ☐ System-generated alerts that highlight areas where orders should be updated even when "locked" by trading partners to meet specified levels of customer service and inventory policy

 ## SUPPLY CHAIN COLLABORATION WITH mySAP SCM*,**

Dirk Kansky
Director Global Solution Marketing, SAP AG

1. Collaboration with mySAP SCM

With the emergence of adaptive supply chain networks, improved collaboration with partners across the network is vital. Without it, suppliers that are further away from end customers suffer because they have no visibility into demand, which means increased variability as information works its way through the network.

To deal with that problem, companies must carry extra inventory and implement time buffers — or run the risk of stock outages. These buffers impair the

---

competitive ability of the overall supply chain network because they create delays and drive up the eventual cost of the end product.

mySAP SCM is a comprehensive supply chain solution that delivers a complete suite of applications for visibility, planning, execution, and collaboration in the entire supply chain network. mySAP SCM enables consumer products companies to anticipate consumer behavior, including the impact of promotions, and to forecast demand more accurately. And it combines distribution and transportation capabilities to support demand-driven replenishment of finished goods in the most profitable way.

With mySAP SCM, SAP provides a collaborative supply chain platform for efficiently integrating all suppliers and customers. It paves the way to real-time synchronization of supply chain processes and facilitates the realization of new supply chain network concepts, such as the demand-driven supply network and fourth-party logistics (4PL). mySAP SCM supports all B2B upstream and downstream initiatives that are in place in several industries, such as the ECR initiative in the consumer products industry.

mySAP SCM collaboration capabilities help business partners work together to reduce inventory buffers, increase the velocity of raw materials and finished goods through the pipeline, improve customer service, and increase revenues.

2. The Key Elements of mySAP SCM for Supply Chain Collaboration

The mySAP SCM supply chain collaboration capabilities include collaborative processes, supply chain application components, and the NetWeaver technology platform.

2.1. Collaborative Processes

mySAP SCM supports inter-enterprise business processes that help improve customer service, increase efficiency, and reduce overall supply chain costs. The following collaborative processes are supported by mySAP SCM.

Responsive replenishment — A new, innovative solution for enhancing the responsiveness of customer-facing collaborative replenishment programs. It addresses the business requirements for consumer products companies and industries with similar downstream distribution structures.

In responsive replenishment, the vendor makes the primary inventory decisions for the customer (the retailer). In addition to the features of classical vendor managed inventory (VMI), the responsive replenishment process within mySAP SCM supports a number of innovative replenishment processes (see also Figure 1). These include:

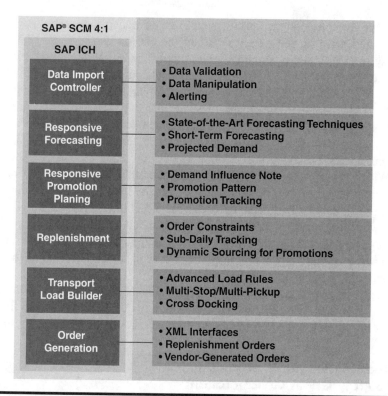

Figure 1. Responsive Replenishment: Functional Building Blocks.

- **Demand driven** — Unlike the traditional, reorder-point-driven VMI process, responsive replenishment is primarily driven by actual demand information sent into the vendor's SAP ICH system by customers. Importing point-of-sale (POS) data significantly enhances overall visibility throughout the supply chain.
- **Out-of-stock driven** — Traditional VMI programs focus on withdrawal and forecasts at the distribution center level, paying no attention to stockouts at the store level. With responsive replenishment, partners can receive out-of-stock information from the store level and execute sales forecasting and promotion planning based on store-level information.
- **Promotion centered** — The responsive replenishment process in mySAP SCM supports a new process to manage and execute promotions jointly. Promotions can be planned and executed separately from day-to-day business and can take retailers' last-minute changes in promotion activities into account.

- **Subdaily** — The entire planning process can be executed in subdaily planning buckets. This allows more adaptive, inventory-reducing replenishment cycles.
- **Optimization of fulfillment** — An amplified, intelligent, replenishment and load-building process optimizes the loading of trucks and minimizes the number of shipments.
- **Data quality oriented** — A data import controller in mySAP SCM handles the data staging, simulation, and correction process.

Collaborative planning, forecasting, and replenishment (CPFR®) — Consumer packaged goods manufacturers face a key challenge today: how to best work with global retailers. Those retailers control the manufacturer's channels to market and they have superior knowledge of consumer behavior. Although manufacturers and retailers share a common interest in creating efficient and adaptive supply chains, a manufacturer has more at risk if things go wrong. When a manufacturer's product is not at the POS, the manufacturer loses the sale. The retailer, on the other hand, usually will not because it can offer consumers a competitor's product.

With the CPFR® capabilities within mySAP SCM, manufacturers and their trading partners can accelerate the speed and accuracy of propagating demand-influencing activities across the supply network. This can be knowledge about promotions, new product introductions, category performance, and so on. By providing each other with visibility into inventory and by collaborating on a single, shared forecast of customer demand, partners can reduce waste and optimize selling opportunities.

In addition, mySAP SCM is certified by the Drummond Group, according to the EAN.UCC CPFR® version 1.3 standard, which means the solution is open and flexible enough to connect with a wide range of customers. With mySAP SCM, CPFR® enables exception-based processes that improve supply chain visibility, enhance trading partner collaboration, and significantly increase efficiency.

Four basic elements make up the overall functionality of CPFR® with mySAP SCM. They are:

1. **Data import controller** — A data import controller handles data staging, simulation, and the correction process. The system can receive and send out sales forecasts, sales forecast revisions, product activity, and retail event messages according to the EAN.UCC CPFR® version 1.3 standard.
2. **Forecast manager** — An automated forecast reconciliation tool intelligently alerts supply chain professionals to exceptions. The forecast

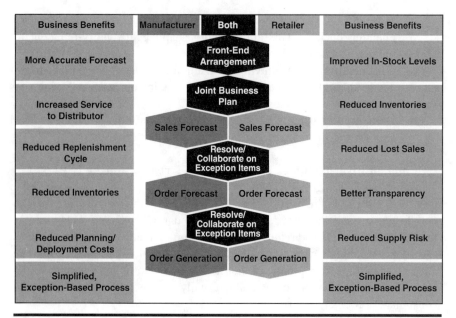

Figure 2. Process Flow of CPFR®.

manager helps companies respond promptly to out-of-tolerance situations before they cause major disruptions.

3. **Order manager** — An automated order-reconciliation process helps ensure smooth supply chain operations.

4. **Exception manager** — A user-friendly, Web-based, task-oriented interface delivers a complete view of all current exceptions along with the corresponding data needed to resolve them.

Through these powerful components, CPFR® with mySAP SCM provides improved visibility into demand and helps companies increase inventory turns by integrating demand and supply-side processes and flawlessly managing variability (see also Figure 2).

Vendor managed inventory (VMI) — The VMI process supports the flow of information and products between manufacturers and retailers (Figure 3). With VMI, the manufacturer proactively manages the inventory at a retailer's site based on a continuous exchange of store-by-store stock levels and sales information between the retailer and the supplier. This process relies on a seamless flow of real demand information, so it shifts the business partners from a buyer-seller relationship to a win-win situation.

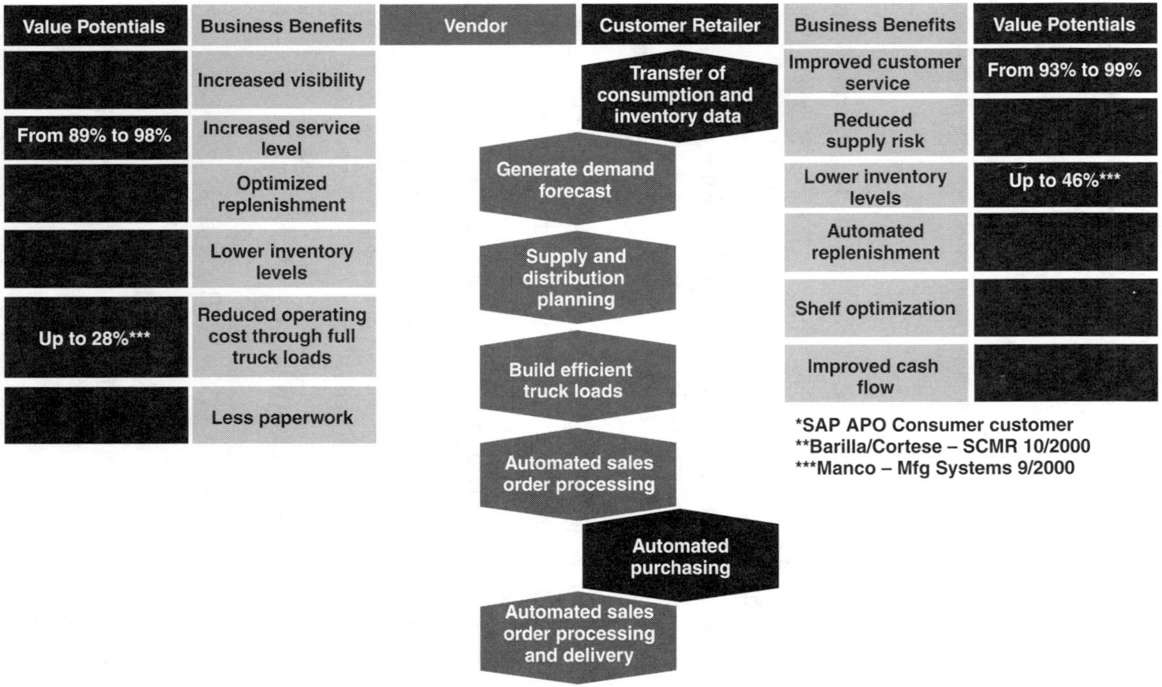

Figure 3. Process Flow of Vendor Managed Inventory (VMI).

VMI can bring significant benefits to both manufacturers and retailers. For consumer products manufacturers, VMI can enable closer relationships with trading partners, improve the visibility of upcoming demand, smooth production due to higher demand visibility, reduce inventory, and increase service levels. For retailers, it can reduce inventory, increase customer service levels, increase inventory turns, reduce fixed assets, reduce stock outages, and increase consumer satisfaction at the POS. mySAP SCM supports VMI and enables partners to see the entire planning process, from sales to production to transport planning.

With mySAP SCM:

- Retailers can send POS data directly to a supplier's SAP demand planning system using EDI (and the Internet in the future). Those data provide the input for the manufacturer's weekly demand planning.
- Promotional business data agreed on by the retailer and manufacturer can be sent and processed individually based on SKUs.
- Once the manufacturer has developed a forecast, a model of the entire supply network and all of its constraints can be built using supply network planning in mySAP SCM and the deployment/transport load builder component of the solution.
- Hundreds of locations, production sites, retailer distribution centers, and retail stores can be viewed using a graphical command center.
- Planning can be performed at both aggregate and detailed levels, taking into account a variety of constraints, such as transportation, warehouse capacity, and production capacity.
- Transportation can be planned with the solution's transport load builder, which optimizes transport loads by grouping available products according to deployment recommendations.
- If direct retail feedback is available, a retail VMI account can be modeled as a customer within mySAP SCM.

Supplier managed inventory (SMI) — The SMI process shifts the responsibility for inventory planning from manufacturer to supplier. The manufacturer moves the responsibility for replenishment to an external business partner, usually the supplier of a product required for the customer's production. This saves effort and also enables the company to take advantage of the business partner's experience in handling replenishment.

In SMI, suppliers determine the shipment schedule based on information provided by manufacturers, such as demand, consumption, and inventory balances. The suppliers have to maintain stock levels at the manufacturer's locations according to contractual agreements. As a result, SMI enhances demand and inventory visibility for suppliers and helps to increase the responsiveness of all parties in the supply chain network.

mySAP SCM enables supply chain partners to:

■ Capture supply opportunities simultaneously
■ Shift the supply chain network from a consumer push focus to a pull focus
■ Enhance supply visibility through real-time information sharing
■ Jointly plan and execute supply chain activities as early as possible
■ React simultaneously and immediately to disruptions in the supply chain
■ Work with integrated data

See the inventory overview example in Figure 4.

2.2. Supply Chain Application Components

SAP Inventory Collaboration Hub (SAP ICH) — By nature, collaborative supply chain processes have special requirements of their software architecture. SAP has therefore designed SAP ICH so that it can be implemented separately from existing internal planning and execution systems, such as SAP APO and mySAP ERP. SAP ICH can also be implemented inside or outside a firewall or in an electronic marketplace (Figure 5).

SAP ICH provides:

■ **Scalability and performance** — It supports simultaneous access by multiple users from different devices and can handle large data volumes in collaborative replenishment scenarios.
■ **User friendliness** — SAP ICH is a Web-based application that is easy to manage with user interfaces that are easy to learn.
■ **Standards compliance** — SAP ICH is based on SAP NetWeaver technology, which uses industry standards. This compliance with global standards means that companies do not have to develop bilateral solutions with each trading partner and can more easily collaborate with a variety of partners.
■ **Data security and integrity** — Because the data exchanged by supply chain members are often very sensitive, SAP ICH provides user authorization and ensures data integrity during transmission.
■ **Self-service and process automation** — SAP ICH is designed to handle all types of collaborative data and information exchange between trad-

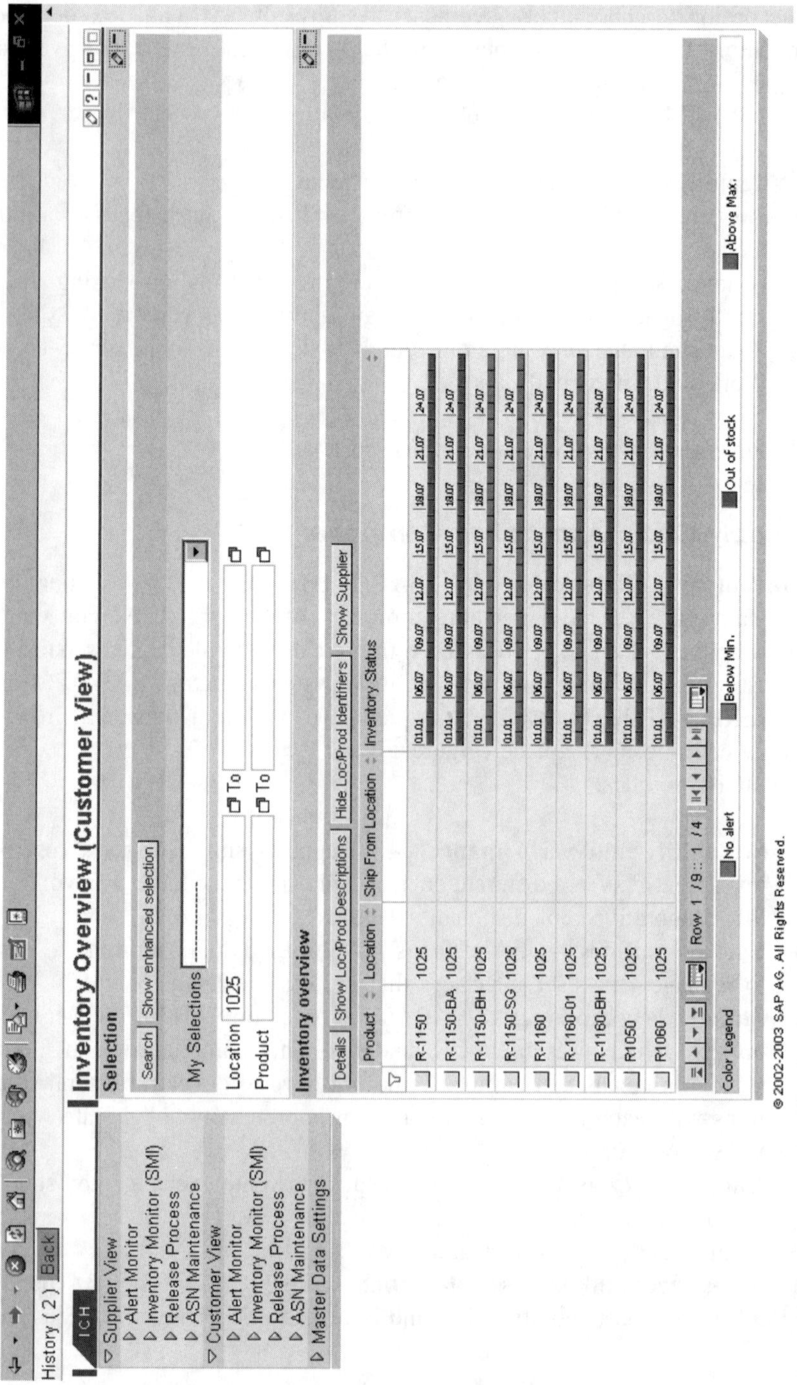

Figure 4. Inventory Overview.

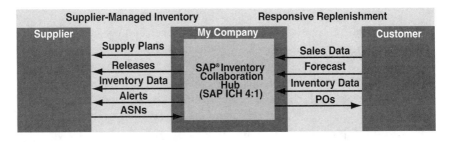

Figure 5.   Collaborative Supply Chain Processes with SAP ICH.

ing partners. Depending on the scenario, SAP ICH enables real-time collaboration, manual self-services, and fully automated scenarios with no intervention by users.

SAP Advanced Planning and Optimization (SAP APO) — SAP APO provides supply chain planning functionality to enable advanced planning processes of organizations across multiple industries. SAP APO offers support for demand, supply, transportation, manufacturing, and strategic planning. It enables companies to gain an end-to-end view of profitable demand and supply resource requirements across an adaptive network. Tight integration of SAP APO with the solution's supply chain execution capabilities facilitates electronic-based order promising, as well as the integration of planning and execution information.

2.3. Supply Chain Collaboration and SAP NetWeaver

SAP's supply chain collaboration components are built entirely on SAP NetWeaver, the application and integration platform based on SAP's Enterprise Service Architecture. Companies can combine mySAP SCM collaboration capabilities with key SAP NetWeaver technologies to further enhance the integration of people and processes through supplier and supply chain portals and multichannel access.

- **Supply chain portal** — Based on the SAP Enterprise Portal component of SAP NetWeaver, the supply chain portal makes it easy to integrate partners into a supply chain network and to enable employees to collaborate with business partners, customers, and coworkers down the hall — or across the globe. Users can work across enterprise boundaries, enabling companies to forge closer relationships with suppliers, partners, and customers. The result is seamless collaboration throughout the entire supply chain network. The portal gives users personalized access to all the information, applications, and services they need to do their jobs. It uses role-based technology to deliver information that is based on users' individual responsibilities within the supply chain network. The supply chain portal helps users avoid being overwhelmed by a flood of irrelevant data, which increases productivity and reduces administrative costs.

■ **Supplier portal** — With the supplier portal, companies can easily combine the capabilities of mySAP Supplier Relationship Management's supplier self-service capabilities to procure indirect materials, services, design, and contracting with the supplier collaboration scenarios offered by mySAP SCM. In addition, companies can enhance the collaborative features of the portal using the mySAP Product Lifecycle Management's collaboration folders (cFolders) capability.

■ **Multichannel access** — The mobile supply chain management capabilities in mySAP SCM enable people throughout the supply chain network to collaborate seamlessly and effectively using mobile and remote devices.

Companies can take advantage of standard protocols, such as Wireless Application Protocol (WAP), i-mode, Bluetooth, and wireless LAN devices. With those technologies, they can perform mobile data entry and automate many data-capture activities in plants and warehouses. And decision makers can gather information and act whether they are on the road, working in a remote facility, or virtually anywhere else. These mobile capabilities increase visibility by enabling information to flow freely from remote end users to the company — from bar code to PDA to enterprise system. Overall, mobile supply chain management reduces information latency and helps increase productivity, improve customer service, and shorten order-to-cash cycles.

See Figure 6 for an example.

3. Outlook

To help companies keep up with the rapidly evolving world of adaptive supply chain networks, SAP continues to expand and strengthen the collaboration capabilities of mySAP SCM. For example, current development efforts are focused on creating an infrastructure that accelerates the integration of enterprise applications, both SAP and non-SAP. SAP and the mySAP SCM solution also continue to support and adhere to common business process standards, such as CPFR® and VMI as defined and developed by the Voluntary Interindustry

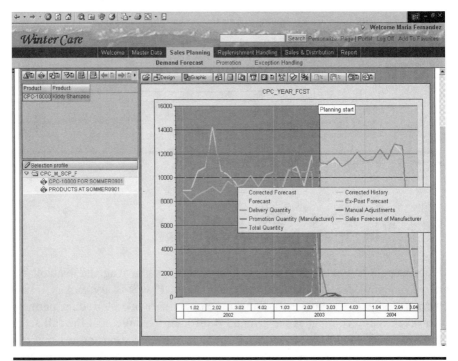

Figure 6. CPFR® Portal.

Commerce Standards (VICS) organization. And SAP is rapidly moving forward with support for the Web services standard — Web Services Descriptive Language (WSDL) — and the XML technical format for message-based interface design and communication.

For now, companies have mostly implemented true collaboration to extend inventory visibility to suppliers and forecasting visibility with customers. However, SAP expects that over time more and more processes will become collaborative and will reach further into the extended supply chain network. More areas of intercompany collaboration will be combined in single processes, and processes will evolve from pure information-sharing activities to more interactive problem and exception resolution.

Collaboration processes will also be extended to a capability known as n-Tier collaboration. n-Tier collaboration gives companies the ability to work with multiple tiers of suppliers and partners, using industry-specific collaborative processes, rather than just first-tier partners that are connected directly to the enterprise (see also Figure 7).

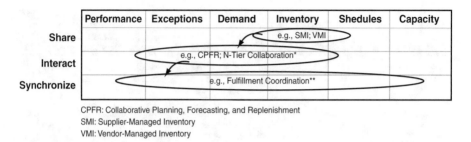

	Performance	Exceptions	Demand	Inventory	Shedules	Capacity
Share				e.g., SMI; VMI		
Interact			e.g., CPFR; N-Tier Collaboration*			
Synchronize			e.g., Fulfillment Coordination**			

CPFR: Collaborative Planning, Forecasting, and Replenishment
SMI: Supplier-Managed Inventory
VMI: Vendor-Managed Inventory

Figure 7.   Evolution of Collaborative Processes.

 **Syncra**   CP, CF, CR:
THE EVOLUTION OF CPFR®

Since its publication in 1998, pundits and practitioners have agreed that collaborative planning, forecasting, and replenishment (CPFR®) is a visionary framework for aligning supply and demand across a network of trading partners. However, many companies have found it difficult to implement the full scope of the CPFR® model. Most successful projects have focused on just one part of CPFR® at a time — the one that offers the highest return on investment for the particular trading relationship.

The VICS CPFR® committee reviewed the issues that had held up CPFR® deployments and developed a new CPFR® model in the spring of 2004 that addressed them. The new model, shown in Figure 1, has many advantages over the original CPFR® framework:

■ **The consumer is at the center of the model**. The goal of collaboration has always been to satisfy consumers with better product availability at lower cost. The new model makes the consumer focus visually apparent.

■ **Collaboration is a continuous cycle of activities**. The old model showed CPFR® as a linear, numbered sequence of steps. However, everyone in a customer/supplier relationship recognizes that companies are always

---

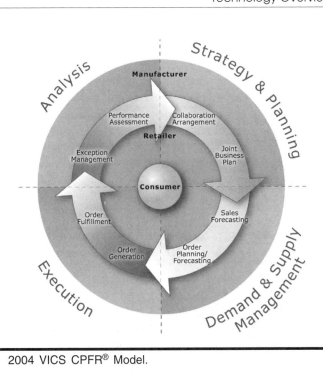

Figure 1.   2004 VICS CPFR® Model.

simultaneously selling products, shipping the next order, and planning the next promotion. The new CPFR® eliminates the presumption that there is a start and finish (or any predetermined order) to this process.

- **Execution and analysis are fundamental to success**. The original CPFR® model supported demand planning and forecasting in great detail, but gave little to no guidance on execution and analysis activities. The nine-step process ended with order commitment; order fulfillment and delivery execution were a footnote. The new model rebalances the CPFR® tasks to encompass execution and place more emphasis on collecting and sharing the performance metrics that measure the success of the initiative.

These improvements make the CPFR® model more understandable, comprehensive, and appealing to different audiences, especially management. However, they do not change how CPFR® is implemented. That is left to CPFR® scenarios, which are more detailed how-to guides to specific "flavors" of CPFR® initiatives. Based on the learnings of successful programs, these scenarios have the biggest potential to enhance a company's collaboration success.

Few companies could or should collaborate in every aspect of their planning, forecasting, and replenishment processes. Manufacturers and retailers in highly promoted channels concentrate their efforts on coordinating retail events to synchronize supply and demand where the volatility (and opportunity for out-of-stocks or overstocks) is greatest. Manufacturers and retailers in everyday low-price (EDLP) channels that have access to high-quality point-of-sale (POS) forecasts have adapted their demand planning processes to support collaborative forecasting. Manufacturers, retailers, and suppliers that have relied on continuous replenishment program (CRP) processes in the past are evolving to collaborative replenishment (CR) initiatives. CPFR® scenarios convert the high-level boxes and arrows pictures of the generic CPFR® model into step-by-step instructions for each of these CPFR® variants.

Collaborative Planning: Synchronizing Promotional Events

In many supply chains, promotional product sales volumes dwarf those during nonpromotional periods. In Europe, nearly 35 percent of retail sales are on promotion. In some countries, the number is even higher — Spanish retailers sell 50 percent of their goods on promotion.*

Collaborating on promotions is essential in these channels, yet projects to date have been limited in scale because there has not been a viable process and data standard for sharing information about them. Some companies share spreadsheets, but these are different for each partner and are impossible to integrate with the systems at each end that plan promotion tactics and volumes.

Major progress on collaborative planning has been made recently. In 2003, EAN International and the Uniform Code Council (UCC) approved the *EAN.UCC XML Retail Event Message* standard. Retailers now have a common, computer-processable format that they can use to communicate promotion details, as well as any changes due to logistics issues, weather, competitive activity, or other factors. The latest round of interoperability testing among leading CPFR® software providers included retail event message interchange, and the message is already in production use.

Meanwhile, a cooperative effort between the VICS CPFR® committee and the UCC Plan Business Requirements Group (BRG) yielded the *Retail Event Collaboration Business Process Guidelines*. This document, available from the CPFR® Web site (www.CPFR.org), presents the business case for collaborating on promotions, identifies the roles and responsibilities of each organization, and describes each step in the process. The guidelines illustrate the data interchange required throughout the life cycle of collaboration and present formulas for key event performance metrics. This first published CPFR® scenario is an excellent starting point for an implementation team that is starting its own corporate initiative.

---

* Accenture, Henkel CPFR Case Study, ECR Europe Presentation, 2002.

Collaborative Planning with Syncra Events™

Manufacturers and retailers typically have planning systems in place to handle promotions, but they have never previously shared much on-line information with trading partners about these events. Beyond simply communicating event details via XML over the Internet, companies need an application that can reconcile local and trading partner views of promotional data.

Syncra Events has been developed to fill the gap between the retailer's need to plan quantities by distribution center and store and the manufacturer's higher-level view of promotions across its markets. The application collects data from enterprise planning applications and trading partners and then integrates the planned impacts with demand and shipment forecasts. Syncra Events tracks milestones and changes as they occur and provides analytical tools to gauge retail event performance.

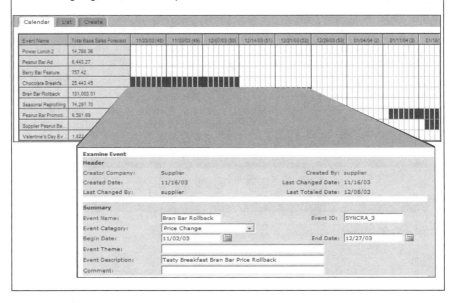

Collaborative Forecasting: Letting Consumers Drive Supply

The consolidation of demand among a small number of ever-growing retailers has increased the importance of individual accounts. Increasingly, high-quality POS data and POS forecasts are available from these retailers. The challenge for manufacturers has been how to leverage these key customer forecasts in the corporate demand planning process. Manufacturers have not previously had an account-specific demand forecast that they could use as a basis for collaboration. As a result, many early CPFR® projects were not integrated with enterprise planning, yielding little inventory benefit for the manufacturer.

Leading manufacturers are adapting their sales and operations planning (S&OP) processes to accommodate retailer-specific forecasts. Instead of driving future plans off of historical shipments data, they are feeding customer-provided POS and POS forecast data for key accounts into their demand plans, using

Collaborative Forecasting with Syncra Demand™

Increasingly, demand planning organizations want to collaborate with other teams in their enterprise, as well as with customers and suppliers. They recognize that to maximize their effectiveness, forecasts must be communicated to all parties that they affect and should incorporate intelligence gathered from many points in the demand chain.

Syncra Demand responds to these contemporary forecasting challenges. Syncra Demand integrates a world-class forecasting engine (Roadmap Technologies' Geneva) with the Syncra Xt™ platform and other Syncra applications. The result is a demand forecasting system that addresses the need for a collaborative account-based planning solution that can incorporate the impact of promotions and can build accurate plans bottom up. Syncra Xt's flexible disaggregation (allocation) features allow users to make adjustments at any level of the product, customer, or local location hierarchies. Customers and suppliers can develop their own separately maintained plans, which can be compared through Syncra Xt exceptions.

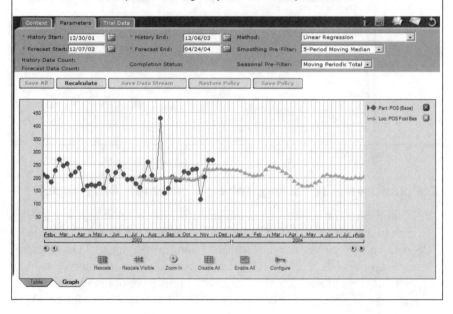

statistical forecasting and replenishment planning tools to align the data with the shipment plans used for the rest of the customers (which remain market based, rather than account specific).

Collaborative forecasting allows manufacturers to build demand plans that take their customers' plans into account and that reflect inventory in the customer's supply chain. Collaborative demand planning is less vulnerable to overstating demand when forward buying or diversion has taken place. The process also yields true account-specific forecasts — the basis for contributing meaningful feedback on customer plans.

Collaborative Replenishment: Continuous Replenishment Programs Come of Age

Continuous replenishment program (CRP) solutions have grown in popularity over the past ten years, particularly in Europe. Typically, CRP delegates the responsibility for calculating replenishment requirements to the supplier. The customer simply provides inventory or distribution center withdrawal information and the supplier calculates required order quantities to keep the customer in stock. In the United States, this process is also sometimes called vendor managed inventory (VMI). Many direct-store-delivery (DSD) programs operate as a CRP as well.

The CRP process is intended to isolate the replenishment calculation from other enterprise processes. The supplier takes on new responsibilities, but does not have to change the order handling or shipment processes used to satisfy demand through other customer channels.

In spite of its popularity, CRP has many flaws. By delegating the responsibility for supply, the customer also gives up control of the process. Customers have little or no visibility to planned shipments. Suppliers, meanwhile, can be caught unprepared by promotions, assortment changes, and other major shifts in demand, due to the short planning horizon that CRP typically uses.

Many organizations have turned to collaborative replenishment as a more balanced approach to CRP initiatives. In collaborative replenishment, both the customer and the supplier have visibility to demand and longer-term forecasts are used to highlight upcoming surges and lulls that call for advanced planning.

Procter & Gamble and Reckitt-Benckiser have both reported major benefits from collaborative replenishment initiatives. Working with eleven suppliers, Procter & Gamble reported a supply-chain-wide inventory reduction of 33 percent; Reckitt-Benckiser reported a 37 percent reduction working with one of its key suppliers. In the retail arena, Superdrug (a U.K.-based health and beauty chain) has experienced improvements in forecast accuracy, in-stock positions, and store-level inventory by using collaborative replenishment.

Collaborative Replenishment with Syncra Supply™

Syncra Supply is a highly flexible, Web-based planning engine that allows manufacturers and retailers to collaborate on the process of turning demand forecasts into replenishment plans. Syncra Supply takes current inventory, safety stock, transit times, shipping and receiving calendars, open orders, and other supply chain data and parameters that trading partners set into account as it projects shipments, receipts, and future inventory positions.

Syncra Supply is an advanced replenishment planning solution because it can use demand forecasts and variable safety stock thresholds to produce highly accurate order plans. These features can lead to dramatically lower inventory requirements to meet the given customer service level, as compared with reorder-point-driven replenishment systems (including most VMI solutions).

Syncra Supply supports collaborative replenishment by giving visibility and planning responsibility to the buyer, the seller, or both, depending on the trading relationship.

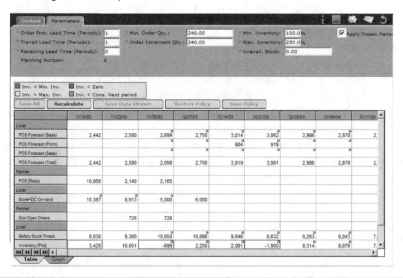

Conclusion

The evolution of CPFR® into specific scenarios for CP, CF, and CR is not a cause for concern, but rather a necessary step in reengineering enterprise processes to take advantage of collaboration. CPFR® has always been a reference model, with many alternatives. Dozens of independent initiatives can fit within the CPFR® theme.

Concentrating on one piece of CPFR® at a time has a silver lining: Once companies have really integrated and leveraged their initial collaborative pro-

---

Syncra Xt: The De Facto Standard for CPFR®

Whatever the CPFR® focus — collaborative planning with a European grocer, collaborative forecasting with a club store chain, or collaborative replenishment with a drug store chain — Syncra has a proven platform: Syncra Xt. Syncra Xt is a common platform that integrates efforts across multiple partners with differing collaboration strategies: CP, CF, CR, and full CPFR®. The Syncra Events, Syncra Demand, and Syncra Supply applications are all tightly integrated with it. As the scope of CPFR® changes or grows, users can simply switch on the applications they require, trading partner by trading partner.

Top retailers and manufacturers worldwide use Syncra Xt. The WorldWide Retail Exchange has standardized on Syncra as its CPFR® solution. Many other companies purchase Syncra for installation in-house or use Syncra's SyncUp hosting service.

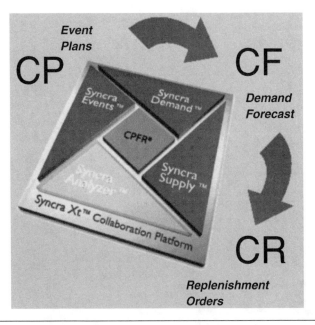

cess, they are well positioned to get even more return on investment from others. The vision of CPFR® will ultimately be achieved through incremental steps. However, viewed across the dozens of key trading relationships that companies have, many may find themselves taking these incremental steps in parallel. It is important to keep the big picture of CPFR® in mind and select processes and technologies that scale across a number of initiatives, even while focusing collaboration efforts.

QUESTIONS

1. What are some of the key benefits that supply chain collaboration software provides?
2. What are the four key components to the VICS CPFR® technology standard?
3. What is a "forecasting warning" signal?
4. What are the three types of "exchanges"?

9

BEST IMPLEMENTATION PRACTICES

In the beginning of this book, we discussed the "lure" of supply chain collaboration as well as the need to smooth out the bullwhip effect caused by a noncollaborative supply chain. The supply chain collaboration best practice, when properly implemented, is the result of several best practices that are implemented together. With the hundreds of successful collaborative relationships as well as the failures, we can always see where the implementation of a best practice or the failure to implement the best practice can be identified. What are some of the key best practices for a successful supply chain collaboration program?

CLASS "A" ALIGNMENT OF PEOPLE, PROCESS, AND TECHNOLOGY

We often look at most major supply chain initiatives as a technology project and fail to see that the majority of the effort should be focused on the business issues (see Figure 42). If we allow for our supply chain collaboration program to exist in this alienated disconnect, then we end up with what is shown in Figure 43.

For many of us who have been in the industry for a long time, this picture looks very familiar. I have seen it over and over again for twenty-five-plus years. We install new technology and we think it becomes the answer to all our troubles. It is only when we align our people and processes with the technology that we can get to the "Class A" performance we can expect with

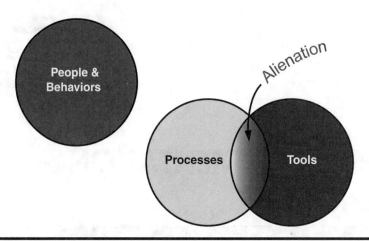

Figure 42.   What Happens When People, Process, and Technology Are Not Integrated. (©2004 Oliver Wight International.)

Old Processes + New Technology = Expensive Old Processes

Figure 43.   What Happens When Behaviors Are Not Changed. (©2004 Oliver Wight International.)

a successful supply chain collaboration program (see Figure 44). It is then that we can smooth the supply chain bullwhip and reap the financial rewards we are expecting.

EDUCATION

Supply chain collaboration education is critical for everyone involved in the process to obtain so they truly understand what collaborative partnerships are and how to implement them. This education should have an 80 percent focus on the business process issues associated with collaborative relations, which would include the cultural, trust, accountability, and organizational, as well as

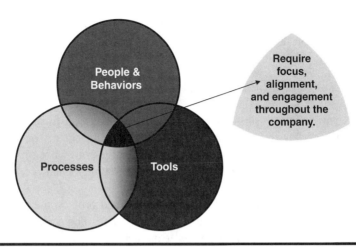

Figure 44.   Class A Collaboration Goal. (©2004 Oliver Wight International.)

the new roles and responsibilities associated with the collaborative relationship. The other 20 percent of the collaborative education should be focused on the technology and how the systems are used for the collaboration process. This includes the forecast generation, the online collaborative screen usage, and the research and reportage tools.

Three common mistakes are often made when it comes to education:

1. **The education focus is on the software with little on the process** — Supply chain collaboration is a transformational strategy and is heavily centered on people and process behaviors. If we fail to educate people properly on the best-practice business process behaviors, we end up making the same old mistakes faster and at a lot more expense.

2. **We educate and then do not use it** — The age-old lesson "if you don't use it, you lose it" holds true here as well. Make sure you tie the education process in with the collaboration process. In addition, education is a journey and should be considered an ongoing process and not just a one-time event

3. **We fail to educate everyone** — Supply chain collaboration impacts almost everyone and so everyone should be educated on the process. It is critical for the executives to be educated, as they are the transformational supporters. It is also critical for all the links in the supply chain to go through an education program, as each functional area will end up with some impact to the program. We are not saying that everyone goes through the same education program, but all should go through a tailored

education that provides an overview of the process as well as their specific role and responsibility.

EXECUTIVE-LEVEL SPONSORSHIP

We have mentioned that supply chain collaboration is a transformational strategy. Because of this transformational impact, the requirement for executive-level sponsorship and leadership is a must. Executives must not only be educated on collaboration, but must also sponsor the supply chain collaboration process as a corporate priority.

The executives need to be the barrier breakers and provide the support and guidance to help break down the barriers of resistance. The collaboration program will encounter many emotions as it impacts the "we have always done it this way" resistance. If executive-level support is lacking, then the chance for success will be limited.

The executives must sponsor the needed changes in:

- Culture
- Organization
- Incentives and rewards
- Technology investments

Finally, the executive must be aligned with the trading partners' executives throughout the supply chain collaborative partnership. We are not saying that they must meet face to face on a regular basis, but they do need to have a mutual understanding of and agreement on the mission of the partnership and the desire to have a win/win business relationship.

TRUST

One of the biggest uncertainties in supply chain collaboration is trust — trust in sharing trading partner data and the trust in people doing what they say they are going to do. There is always a risk associated with the trust issue, and you have to weigh this risk against the potential rewards that can be obtained by having a best-practice collaboration program. There is the risk of sharing data and the risk of not sharing data. Sam Walton, founder of Wal-Mart, said it well back in 1988, as shown in Figure 45.

It was this direction by Sam that sent the Wal-Mart technology team on a mission to develop the private exchange used today, Retail Link, and to add additional electronic data interchange inbound and outbound capabilities. But

"COMMUNICATE everything you possibly can to your partners. The more they know, the more they'll understand. The more they understand, the more they'll care. Once they care, there's no stopping them"

— **Sam Walton**, founder of Wal-Mart Stores, Inc.
Made in America – My Story

Figure 45. Sam Walton on Communication. (©2004 Oliver Wight International.)

even with this openness to sharing data with its trading partner vendors, Wal-Mart continues to control risks. For example, all the Wal-Mart information shared with trading partners must either remain in the Wal-Mart Retail Link system or stay behind a vendor's own firewall. The data are not allowed to be on a third-party's server, for example, on a public exchange.

Because of this fear of the risk of losing control of the Wal-Mart data, many onsite vendor teams refuse to share the data internally with their own corporate headquarters and manufacturing processing. This lack of trust, internally, has become a great inhibitor to reaping the significant benefits that a good supply chain collaboration can have in smoothing the bullwhip and leverage to supply chain visibility that could be available.

Former Wal-Mart President Bill Fields used to quote a good rule: "Trust, but verify"; trust people and the processes, but also put in the checks and balances that will verify that the process is working.

Trusting people to do what they say they are going to do is also an issue. People will often look at what is best for them as individuals or for their own functional silos and not look at the bigger picture of what their actions could cause. This behavior is often one of the major causes of the bullwhip effect. The incentives and performance metrics that encourage and reward people to behave in a most trustworthy manner need to be provided. In many cases, people are rewarded to behave the way they do.

GET CLOSE TO THE CUSTOMER

Another suggested best practice is to have a customer-centric focus. Call it bottom-up planning, demand planning, or pull-based replenishment. Regardless of what we call it, we need to focus on the customer demand to plan our business. Recall the bullwhip chart showed earlier, where the customer demand was fairly smooth and predictable. It was when it traveled down the supply chain pipeline that we saw the roller coaster effect take place as we ignored, lacked the visibility, or failed to see the value in using the demand forecast of the customer.

Another best practice is to take the collaboration visibility down as low in the supply chain as you can, down to the end consumer. Remember that the consumer does not shop in a distribution center. This is not to suggest that you need to collaborate at the store level as much as have the drill-down capability to the store and the systems that can assist in managing at this level through the exception alerts discussed in the technology chapter of this book.

In the Warner-Lambert and Wal-Mart CFAR pilot discussed earlier, we saw a significant disconnect in the aggregated store-level demand versus the actual rebuys done at the distribution centers. We could notice that disconnect because we had visibility to the store-level information. There have also been promotions that were purchased by the retail buyers and shipped to the distribution centers only not to be sent from there to the stores. Sure, we could blame the retailer for the mistake, but in a best-practice collaboration program with the ability to provide visibility to the consumer level, the mistake could have been prevented. You could think of it as vendor managed inventory "plus." It is worth the investment and will significantly reduce inventory and increase sales revenue.

One of Sam Walton's old sayings applies: "If you mine your pennies, the dollars will take care of themselves."

COMMUNICATE AND EXECUTE: INTERNALIZE THE TRADING PARTNER DATA

Supply chain collaboration is not new. We have been communicating for years with our trading partners, but in many ways we have failed to execute well. "Actions speak louder than words," as the old saying goes. When we look at supply chain collaboration, we will often say that it just makes plain old common sense. It does work well if we actually execute it. We use the trading partner collaborated data to run our business process and functions. If we fail to use the information to help drive efficiencies in our processing, then we will fail to obtain the value we could realize.

Earlier, the need for executive sponsorship was mentioned. In most cases, executives report to board members and the shareholders. What is most important to the board members and shareholders is profit. If we fail to utilize the more accurate collaborated information to run our business, then we are failing to increase the profit potential for our company, thus impacting our shareholder boss. Do not just talk about it; follow through and execute by following the collaboration throughout the entire supply chain process.

QUESTIONS

1. What is Class A?
2. What are the three most common failures of education?
3. Why is executive-level sponsorship important?

10

CASE EXAMPLES: RESOLVE CONFLICTS, LEVERAGE OPPORTUNITIES, AND MINIMIZE RISKS

With hundreds of formal supply chain collaborations taking place (Wal-Mart recently announced that 1,200 of its vendors are on CPFR® programs), many companies have discovered lessons learned that were expected as well as unexpected. Supply chain collaboration programs open the door for change. If yours is a company that has been stuck in the struggle of "we have always done it that way" or "our trading partners will never change," here is the opportunity to change that, at an acceptable pace and level that are best suited for you and your trading partners. You can learn by actually doing something about it instead of just studying it. Below are some real-world case examples of companies we have worked with and some of their lessons learned. We have purposely protected the names of the companies, but trust us, these are real companies with real issues.

RESOLVING CONFLICTS

Conflict typically arouses a lot of emotions. However, in many cases, these emotions are justified as we have rewarded and supported this behavior for years. We tend to get emotional when we believe we are doing our job correctly and someone does not like the results. This causes the conflict. We, as well as others, have found that implementing supply chain collaboration causes change or requires making some adjustments to how we have run the business in the past. Roles, behaviors, and performance metrics must be modified, along with the associated incentives to support the collaborative transformation that takes a look at not only individual performances but at the performance of the entire supply chain team.

The conflict in supply chain collaboration can come from external trading partners as well as from our internal partners. The conflicts seen most often in supply chain collaboration have been centered around the "I win, you figure out how to win" mentality. We have observed that this self-centered behavior has been supported and encouraged by corporate policies for years. We have seen individual poor performances and behaviors, but what we really want to address and help to resolve is the much bigger issue of changing corporate and supply chain practices. Conflicts that prevent effective and profitable collaboration through teamwork as well as individual performance to support the overall balanced goals are what need to be resolved.

Let's first take a look at the conflicts we cause in our own backyard. We have mentioned before, and several companies have reported as well, that in many cases, internal collaboration is the hardest to execute. Internal conflicts are seen most often. In fact, collaborating with the trading partner is often easier than collaborating internally. It can be compared to family members who argue most frequently with each other. Supply chain collaboration requires us to review our organizational silos — the roles, responsibilities, and performance measurements that we have developed and supported over many years. It is difficult to modify this culture and organizational establishment and, thus, supports the fact that you must have executive-level support in order to ensure the success of a collaboration program.

We worked with a Fortune 500 consumer packaged goods company whose sales organization was not responsible or held accountable for supply chain initiatives. Like most consumer packaged goods companies, the sales team's primary role was to increase sales revenue and make sure the customer was happy. After all, the sales organization was not typically rewarded on supply chain profitability, as that was someone else's responsibility. In essence, the supply chain was the tail of the dog and frequently tended to be in a reactive mode of operating. The attitude of the sales team was, "We will do whatever it takes to drive sales revenue, and you at corporate need to react, no matter what the cost is, to satisfy our sales-revenue-generating demands and to satisfy the customer."

In this case example, the retail "800-pound gorilla" approached the vendor supply account sales team with an ultimatum, which in itself does not seem very collaborative. "We want you to do a CPFR® program with us," was the message sent from this major retailer to the vendor. This is typically the case with many new industry initiatives; they are normally driven by an industry gorilla, which immediately creates suspicion among the vendors, who may consider themselves victims in these situations. Now the sales organization has to react to this request from the retail customer, and it has to do with something other than just driving sales revenue growth. It has to do with supply chain. What the sales account team did was to turn it over to the corporate headquarters supply chain team to handle and said, "This is your opportunity, as we have nothing to do with supply chain."

The vendor's supply chain team approached the retailer's forecasting and replenishment team to find out exactly what this CPFR® program was. They realized immediately that they were going to have three primary concerns (or, better yet, conflicts) to deal with:

1. How to handle the self-inflicted bullwhip surprises they sometimes encounter from their own internal sales organization driving demand.
2. How to handle the retailer's own internal collaboration issues with the buying organization, which coincidently felt just like the vendor sales-person who had no responsibility or accountability for supply chain costs.
3. How to address the external conflicts that can be caused by the retailer's last-minute demands and changes that dramatically impact the manufacturer's supply chain, creating weeks and months in long-term commitments.

To help surface these concerns, the two trading partner collaboration teams discussed them in the initial joint planning meetings. The challenge was not with those in attendance at the meetings, but with those who felt that they did not need to be part of the collaboration exercise. Not represented in the joint trading partner meetings were the two most critical functions: the salesperson and the merchandise buyer. Neither felt that they had a role in "supply chain" collaboration, yet we have seen both cause the bullwhip effect that we would like to smooth out by improving collaboration.

The team members knew that they had issues to address, but decided to proceed with the CPFR® effort and establish a formal and detailed documentation effort in the pilot experience. They decided that if they could document the facts and let the facts speak for themselves, then maybe they could address the emotional confrontations and resolve them to achieve a win/win situation for everyone's benefit. The joint team did a good job of documenting the roles and responsibilities as well as the performance goals and objectives of the CPFR® pilot and shared this information with their own executive management.

The twelve-week CPFR® pilot was initiated, and great results were obtained immediately as basic replenishment forecast improvements were identified to be causal factors for the product seasonality. In addition, the forecasted demand was shared within the vendor's organization to help better plan manufacturing as well as transportation. Occasionally, some errors were identified ahead of time when products were inadvertently deactivated for replenishment at some retail stores by a replenishment assistant. Needless to say, both sides were happy with the initial results of the pilot. But then came the conflict, or rather conflicts.

A promotional event was going to be offered by the vendor, and the salesperson worked with the buyer to increase the promoted product demand by 70 percent. In the past, similar promotions demonstrated that actual sales demand increased an average of 30 percent. Neither the salesperson nor the buyer wanted to take the chance of running out of product, so they would always order too much product and then return the excess or mark it down. For the supply chain organizations to have too much product meant they had too much inventory, transportation costs, labor-handling costs, and returns. This cost was not just one-sided; it impacted both organizations. The collaboration conflict issue arose because neither the salesperson nor the buyer was going to budge from the "we can't afford to run out of product" protection clause, and neither one had any incentive or reason not to do what they had always done — drive sales. The conflict was more of a frustration from the supply chain participants, as the dominant organizations are sales and merchandising.

The promotional event took place, and sales came in at the 30 percent increase, as had happened in the past. But in this case, the detailed documentation removed the emotion from the assessment and replaced it with fact. This caught the attention of management on both sides, who could actually see the true metrics and the resulting documented costs of the excess inventory, transportation, and labor. It was not so much that the 30 percent was the correct number as it was that the 70 percent promotional lift was excessive. Collaborating to a closer single number was the issue, as neither company wanted to run out of product for the promotion, but rather wanted to have the right amount of product and leverage the knowledge of multiple inputs.

The resolution to the conflict was to balance the metrics and incentives to make sure that everyone had "skin in the game." We still need to drive sales, but we want to drive them so they maximize profits, creating a win/win situation. Using facts and strong documentation of the process was the most important factor. The second most important factor was to have executive management support to ensure that change took place.

LEVERAGE OPPORTUNITIES

Collaboration that drives companies to focus on core competencies is a great way to leverage opportunities. If I bring a transportation company into a collaborative arrangement and let them teach me their business and I teach them my business, together we can most likely identify some opportunities for improvement.

During one of the first collaboration rollouts, we brought in a transportation provider who worked with the teams on what information they could leverage in order to optimize their own transportation efficiencies. We were told that if we could provide them a fairly accurate forecast of shipments to a specific ship-to location two weeks in advance, then they could optimize their drivers. This could save overtime costs as well as reduce the need for many of the drivers to work on weekends and be away from home more days. We were also told that if we could provide the transportation company with forecasts four weeks in advance, they could do a better job of managing the tractors, which would bring significant cost reductions in equipment. Finally, we were told that if we could provide them with a forecast six weeks out, then management of backhauls could be improved by reducing the transportation of partial truck loads or, even worse, empty trucks.

The team took the logistics challenge and began sharing forecasted demand with the transportation company. Some benefits were anticipated, but the bigger benefit came unexpectedly, as with most pilots. The unexpected lesson "learned" was that the retail partner rolled out an automated store-level replenishment system. The increase in sales demand and the resulting order demand was a shock not only to the vendors, but also to the transportation company. Increased demand for products and logistics services immediately caused the transportation company to raise a red flag to let everyone know that they had a constraint. This red flag also caught the attention of many vendors, who also raised their own flags to signal that they were going to have constraints. Because of the collaboration exercise and the simple sharing of forecasted demand, certain adjustments were made to help satisfy as much of the next demand as possible. The retailer also adjusted their rollout strategy collaboratively so the supply chain could handle the additional demand.

Lessons are learned when we share information with our trading partners and give them the authority to do something with it, thus enabling us to optimize our supply chain. We found in this example that if we had gone out even further in supply chain visibility, we could have done even more optimization and been able to handle the replenishment program rollout more aggressively.

MINIMIZE RISKS

As mentioned earlier, Bill Fields, former Wal-Mart president, once told me, "Trust, but verify." This is one way to minimize risk. Trust people to do their jobs correctly, but also have the checks and balances in place to verify that jobs are being done correctly. The risk in sharing information is that it may leak out, but there is also a risk in not sharing information with trading partners and, therefore, losing the potential benefits of collaboration. What is the correct balance to risk? How do you take advantage of the opportunities and benefits that a trading partner collaboration program can provide and minimize your risk while doing so?

We recently worked with a pharmaceutical company whose way of dealing with risk was to always say NO to any new idea. This mind-set was not limited to supply chain initiatives, but was ingrained in the culture of the company. Let's face it, NO is the easiest word in the dictionary to pronounce and hide behind. Just say "NO" and the problem goes away.

The company had one core product that has been a "classic" for it for years, and that was sufficient. "Why rock the boat?" could have been the company's motto. Avoiding mistakes was the top priority for the company, so if it just maintained the status quo, then everything should be fine. This would be true if the world stood still, but in today's world, you cannot afford to risk becoming stagnant. In today's highly competitive world, to rely on what you have always done and refuse to look at ways to improve is a big risk to take. A question we often ask is: "Do you know who your competitors are today and, more importantly, tomorrow?" The emergence of Amazon.com is a good example of current competition that, until just a few years ago, did not exist. Some of Amazon.com's competitors probably did not have the company on their own radar screens.

The pharmaceutical company was suffering from one major issue: profit, or the lack it. To put into one word a theme for what this company was experiencing, that word would be "increasing." Sales were increasing, but lost sales were also increasing. Inventory levels were increasing, inventory carrying costs were increasing, transportation costs were increasing, manufacturing costs were increasing, and labor costs were increasing.

What was confusing for the company was that its forecast was just as accurate as it had always been. The company planned the demand for its product at a corporate level based on global population growth data. This is the way it always planned. What was killing the profits was not the total amount of product the company was making; it was not knowing where the product was going to be consumed or when. This company was in reaction mode all the time, as it was constantly being faced with surprises.

What we uncovered in this "risk-adverse" company was the lack of information sharing between departments. No one trusted anyone else. The culture of the company was that individuals wore blinders and were to focus only on doing their own job without regard for the rest of the company. There was no collaboration, and that prevented process improvement. While interviewing team members, we were not surprised to find out where their pain was coming from. It was the typical business processing adjustments that we see in a demand pull-based environment; the retailer has a promotion, does a major category module reset, or may even add a private-label, competitive product. The issue with this company was that none of the information regarding these changes was shared within the company among the functional areas.

As we continued to reveal the reasons for the lack of information sharing between departments, it boiled down to a lack of trust between corporate departments; no one knew how the data could be used by the other departments. The biggest issue was the fear that the information might leak out to competitors. It was, once again, easier to say "NO" than to actually solve the problem, even as the company was bleeding to death.

How did the company solve this issue of minimizing the risk and then transform to an information-sharing collaborative company? It started by conducting an internal supply chain collaboration project. The least risky was to focus on its own backyard and see if it could just collaborate better as a company. It executed the various core and basic collaborative steps already discussed in this book. Technology was also kept to a minimum in order to maintain a primary focus on the business people and process issues. What was also found during the cross-functional collaborative team workshops was that much of the trading partner data needed to help plan the supply chain better and not be so reactive was already available; one department was collecting the data, but had just never shared it with anyone else within the company.

The cross-functional collaborative workshops resulted in the following outcomes:

- Internal front-end arrangement.
- An internal joint business plan.
- The sharing of trading partner data such as demand forecasts, inventory levels, and scorecards.
- Internal goals with balanced individual, team, and corporate incentives.

- An internally generated, bottom-up, pull-based forecast that was then collaborated with the traditional, top-down, pushed-based forecast. Major gaps in the difference of the forecasts were collaborated among the cross-functional team members to come up with a single consensus forecast number with which to execute the business.

Without ever collaborating with an external trading partner, this company transformed itself through a fairly low-risk approach. The benefits were immediately realized. The new word to describe the company became "reduced."

- Lost sales were reduced by 15 percent.
- Inventory was reduced by 35 percent.
- Transportation costs were reduced by 12 percent.

One other side benefit was experienced by the CEO; he was no longer surprised at the end of the quarter with unexpected financial results. The company's next step: trading partner collaboration.

QUESTIONS

1. What are the two types of collaborative conflicts?
2. Can you cite examples of the two types of collaborative conflicts?
3. Why is it important to document collaborative arrangements and joint business plans?
4. Why is being risk adverse a risk in itself?

11

INTERNALIZING TRADING PARTNER DATA

The true value of supply chain collaboration comes when the information is actually used to execute business. "Actions speak louder than words" is what internalizing trading partner data is all about. We often hear people say that they have been collaborating for years, but many times it means that they have just been talking for years, which does not necessarily mean that it has led to supply chain execution. This is why we have said that the most difficult partner of supply chain collaboration is internal. So what kind of issues have we seen with internalizing trading partner data? The most typical issues are shown in Figure 46.

As you can see, many of the issues involve the people and process change management difficulties that may exist. The issue also may involve technology and, in many cases, lack of understanding of the value in sharing the trading partner information.

George Palmatier, author of the book *Enterprise Sales and Operations Planning* and a senior principal for Oliver Wight Americas, Inc., described the internalizing of trading partner data as the "pitch and the catch." Traditionally, one trading partner throws or passes the information for the other trading partner to catch. The important part is what the catcher does with this valuable information. In many cases, we fail to involve the other players on our team, and the pitching and catching only involves two people. We fail to share this wealth of information with the rest of our supply chain team members, often leaving them in the dark.

- Cultural
- Organizational
- Trust
- Awareness
- Change management
- Technology
- Lack of critical mass
- Excuses
- Not a priority

Figure 46. Issues with Internalizing Trading Partner Data. (©2004 Oliver Wight International.)

The limited trading partner collaboration can be described as "pseudocollaboration," as depicted in Figure 47. As you can see from the illustration, we typically see collaboration occurring between the sales organization and the buying organization. However, this limited collaboration does not involve the rest of the supply chain members, resulting in a less than efficient process that often results in breakdowns. It is not uncommon for us to hear people we have

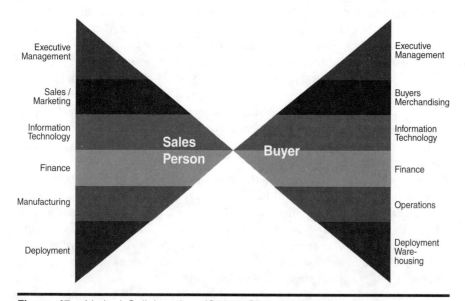

Figure 47. Limited Collaboration. (©2004 Oliver Wight International.)

- Sales and order forecasts
- Product seasonality profiles
- Supply commitments and constraints
- Point of sale, POS
- Shipments and withdrawals
- Inventory positions
- Promotional events
- Marketing plans
- Performance scorecards

Figure 48. Types of Key Trading Partner Data. (©2004 Oliver Wight International.)

interviewed concerning the opportunities they have in running an efficient supply chain comment on how often they are surprised and forced into a reaction mode. These same people will often blame the trading partner for the surprise, but in reality, the trading partner often did communicate the event. It is simply that this "catcher" failed to share the information with anyone else on his or her own internal team. Information that is commonly shared between trading partners is shown in Figure 48. This same information is often shared electronically through the various methods shown in Figure 49.

Why is it, then, that we fail to share trading partner information internally? Most often it is because we do not understand who else needs to know the information so they can process the new data proactively. We often work in our

- EDI
  - 830 – forecast
  - 852 – sales revenue
- EDI AS2
  - EDI using the Internet
- XML
  - Internet based standards B2B
- Exchanges
  - Private
  - Public

Figure 49. Methods for Sharing Trading Partner Information.

own internal silos and ignore the rest of our own internal supply chain, as it is not seen as any of our business or concern. We may also leverage a sequential internal supply chain process instead of a cross-functional supply chain model, and the information is then transposed or lost in the translations as it is passed from function to function.

In many cases, we do not share trading partner information internally because we do not trust our own people. This especially occurs when the customer facing team, typically the sales organization, meets with the buying organization of the trading partner. The entire incentive of the sales organization is to keep the customer happy and drive for increased sales revenue. When they contact the corporate support teams, they want them to react to the needs of the customer. React "now," not later. As we have described before in this book, the customer facing teams are often not measured on profitability or supply chain efficiencies, so they lack motivation or fail to see the value in sharing trading partner data with corporate support people. However, they do have legitimate fears in sharing the information with the corporate support teams: fear that the data will not be used appropriately and fear that the sensitive trading partner data will be leaked to the trading partner's competitors.

The sales organization understands the need to keep the customer's information confidential; such information includes the customer's promotional plans, special buys, pricing strategies, category assortments, growth plans, marketing, as well as other competitive sensitive information. If this information gets into the wrong hands, then strong consequences could occur. This risk of having the data leaked out is often seen as not worth taking the risk.

However, there is the other side of the coin to remember, and that is the risk of not sharing the important trading partner information in order to better execute the supply chain. If the customer fails to get the products in time or your own company is not as profitable as it should be, you need to reassess the value of sharing the information internally and how you can make sure the information is used appropriately. You can do so by collaborating better internally and documenting information confidentiality agreements. In short, you could develop your own internal supply chain collaboration program with the same agreements and understandings that you would adhere to with an external trading partner.

Another important process for internalizing trading partner data is to align your internal supply chain team with the external trading partner's team so the gaps with the information sharing are closed. Figure 50 depicts this alignment.

In this illustration, having the executives of the company aligned is important as they can have the high-level understandings and agreements in a win/win collaborative partnership. By having the other supply chain functions aligned,

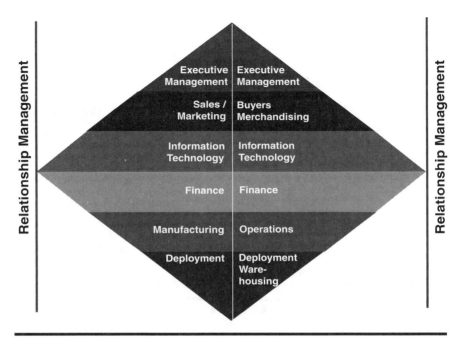

Figure 50.   The Most Effective Collaborative Alignment. (©2004 Oliver Wight International.)

the information sharing is performed between the teams that actually need the information and will perform the execution functions. The "pitch and catch" now involves the entire supply chain and we are operating with a more highly effective team.

INTERNALIZING CUSTOMER DATA INTO MANUFACTURING

Some of the greatest value for internalizing customer data is within the manufacturing planning functions. Processes such as demand planning as well as sales and operations planning are driven by knowing what the customer's forecasted needs are. Many companies will obtain this information from the internal customer facing teams such as from sales; however, it is often found that collaborated customer information is more accurate. For example, CPFR® collaborated forecasts are excellent forms of information to input into the manufacturer's planning processes. Figure 51 depicts how this information can flow into the manufacturer's planning processes.

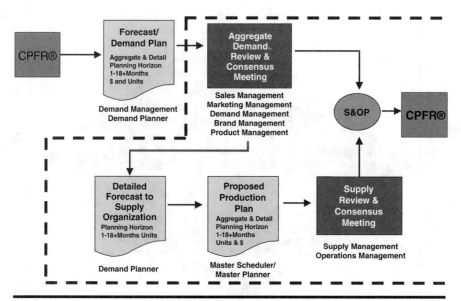

Figure 51. CPFR® Input into Manufacturer's Planning Processes. (©2004 Oliver Wight International.)

The illustration also demonstrates an important output flow of information that goes back to the CPFR® process. This information could be a collaborative response to the trading partner of a manufacturing supply constraint or perhaps an optimization opportunity. This extended supply chain enterprise can now leverage a two-way flow of information between trading partners that now can better manage the supply chain for both product demand as well as product supply. With this new set of information, the upstream trading partner now has an opportunity to make decisions it may never have had the chance to make. For example, if there is a product constraint, the customer may now have the opportunity to plan where the product that is available should be shipped. If the manufacturer has some optimization opportunities, the customer may elect to delay a shipment in order to get a better price point on the product or perhaps save cost in transportation.

The value of internalizing trading partner data has to be considered one of the greatest benefits of supply chain collaboration and yet is rarely adopted today. Systems can no longer be used as the excuse for not internalizing the information. We must address the people and process issues and establish our own internal collaborative programs that will support the effective "pitching and catching" of trading partner data for an overall team win.

QUESTIONS

1. What is the "pitch" and the "catch"?
2. What is "pseudocollaboration"?
3. What are the major processes used for internal collaboration?
4. How are trading partner data shared electronically?

12

EXPERIENCES IN OPTIMIZING A VALUE CHAIN WITH MULTIPLE TRADING PARTNERS

During the original CFAR proof-of-concept pilot between Wal-Mart and Warner-Lambert, the strategic vision was to extend the trading partner collaboration beyond the one-on-one relationship to all the links in the value chain. We called the extended enterprise collaboration CFAR'ther to refer to the extended supply chain visibility that would link the entire supply chain with a single, common forecast number with which to execute. The idea was that if we could share and collaborate on a single forecast number of demand with each function in the supply chain adding its own expertise to make the number more accurate, then we could have a highly efficient and effective extended supply chain. The concept was not only to make the demand drivers more accurate, but also to provide the needed information on supply constraints as well as optimization opportunities.

During the CFAR proof-of-pilot design process, a transportation company was interviewed to see what it would do if part of a CFAR'ther process pilot. We were told that if we could provide the company with an accurate forecast of shipping demand two weeks out, it could optimize its drivers. If we could provide an accurate forecast six weeks ahead of time, it could optimize its trailers.

Today, the term CFAR'ther is no longer used. Two VICS CPFR® subcommittees have been formed to address the collaboration opportunities between

153

multiple trading partners. The CPFR® n-Tier committee is focused on collaborative standards and guidelines between the multiple-tier levels in a supply chain. The VICS mission statement for n-Tier is simple:

> To extend CPFR® to support collaboration across all tiers of the value chain.

The Collaborative Transportation Subcommittee is focused on the logistics side of the supply chain to provide collaborative standards to help improve efficiencies in this industry. What this committee has observed is the significant opportunities that can be revealed through better planning and optimization of freight movement. In many cases, the greatest financial returns in supply chain collaboration may be found in the area of transportation as less than truck loads (LTLs) are minimized and expedited freight costs are reduced.

In many supply chains, the weakest link and perhaps the greatest opportunity is with the partnerships between manufacturing, raw material providers, packing material, copackers, and component suppliers. We often hear that it is much easier to collaborate between a retail customer and its vendors than between a vendor and its own suppliers of product. Why is this? There can be many reasons. According to the VICS CPFR® n-Tier Committee's document, "CPFR® n-Tier Case Studies and Performance Measures," provided to us by chairman Jack Haedicke:

> The downstream portion of the supply chain (between manufacturers and distributors) has long been hampered by distrust and counter-productive supply chain activities (diverting, forward buying, inside margin and trade deal funding). This is a situation that has existed for several decades, and there is no reason to believe that it will change in the near future.

We have also observed that the downstream suppliers tend to be less sophisticated when it comes to business technology systems as well as business processes. For many of these downstream suppliers, they simply make as much as they can with very little visibility of the actual demand for the product. They tend to use past shipments for demand visibility and do not realize the true sales demand for their products and services.

While working with one major consumer package goods manufacturer, we were told that its greatest headaches came from two of its suppliers. One supplier of plastic resin had caused the company not to be able to produce plastic bottles for its core product, resulting in lost sales for two weeks. The other supplier, a producer of bottle labels, was unable to provide the labels in a timely manner, also causing significant lost sales.

The opportunities for supply chain collaboration between suppliers and manufacturers have become so significant that the public exchange Transora, which has a membership of over fifty companies primarily in the consumer packaged goods industry, has decided to focus most of the CPFR® collaborations between suppliers and manufacturers.

n-TIER

Below is the documentation provided to us with permission from Jack Haedicke, chairman of the VICS CPFR® n-Tier subcommittee, describing how they are defining the industry standard guidelines for multiple trading partner supply chain collaboration:

n-Tier

n-Tier is a simple concept. By sharing additional information between additional layers or tiers of a value chain, benefits should accrue to those that are sharing and are in receipt of the shared information based on some "network effect." In other words, each additional "node" or tier that is added should increase the mutual benefit far in excess of the value of the node itself.

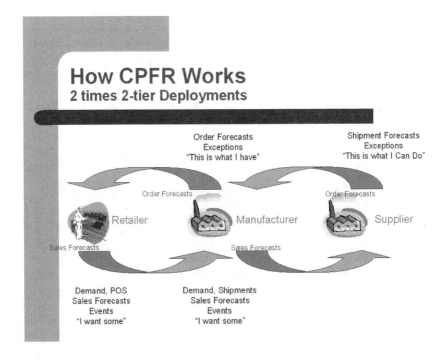

There are several forms of n-Tier CPFR. They include the following:

- Two-tier CPFR between a buyer and seller (the current and previous model)
- Three-tier CPFR between a buyer, seller and the supplier to the seller n-Tier CPFR where any number of buyers and sellers are in a deep, vertical value chain alignment

n-Tier Applicability

The following are examples of products and processes where n-Tier CPFR appears to add value. These are:

- Products Requiring Critical Ingredients
- Primary Packaging Materials
- Secondary Packaging Materials (for transportation)
- Private Label Products
- Highly Promotional or Fashion Products
- New Item Introduction, Product Change, Replacement
- Highly Seasonal
- Strategic Products
- MTO, ETO: High Tech, Automotive, Contract Manufacturing

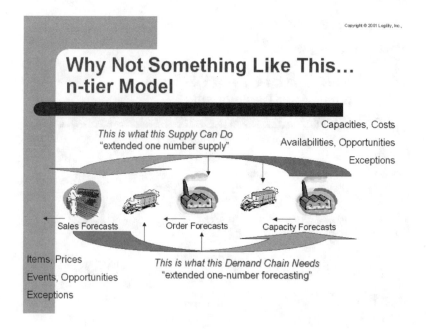

Copyright © 2001 Logility, Inc.,

Why Not Something Like This... n-tier Model

This is what this Supply Can Do "extended one number supply"

Capacities, Costs
Availabilities, Opportunities
Exceptions

Sales Forecasts   Order Forecasts   Capacity Forecasts

Items, Prices
Events, Opportunities
Exceptions

This is what this Demand Chain Needs "extended one-number forecasting"

This model (shown on the previous page) simply extends the principle of three-tier CPFR to include any number of buyers and sellers in a deep, richly collaborative value chain. The model might look as though the value chain is a linear arrangement. However, that is more for conventional presentation. Generally most people would draw such a value chain more as a value web; as though all members have the ability to work together. Each company works in their own series of concentric rings or webs with key strategic partners, second tier, and third tier partners, and so on.

MULTIPLE TRADING PARTNER COLLABORATIONS IN DIFFERENT INDUSTRIES

Multiple trading partner collaborations apply to many industries and best practices. The high-technology sector uses a governing body called RossettaNet that has, for many years, established industry collaboration guidelines with its trading partners. This collaboration is critical in the high-tech industry, as collaborative designs are jointly developed for computer hardware and short-shelf-life products often go out of date in a matter of a few weeks or months.

Supplier relationship management (SRM) is also becoming an industry best practice in supply chain collaborations between manufacturer buyers and supplier providers. They often drive collaborative procurement through the practices of lean manufacturing and kanban utilization. We have recently seen many of the leading technology providers add SRM functionality to their software solutions.

Industries (such as automotive, aerospace, and industrial manufacturing) are also developing supplier portals for collaboration with downstream supply chain partners using what we may define as co-managed, proprietary, and private exchanges. All of these industries see the needs and the benefits of multipartner collaboration, and we believe we have just seen this begin to emerge as a best practice, where most of the focus in collaboration has been centered upstream between the retailers and tier-one manufacturers. It is our opinion that once the lower tiers in the supply chain are better synchronized in the extended supply chain and we see better internalization of trading partner data into sales and operations planning, as described in Chapter 11, the cost of goods sold through manufacturing and logistics optimizations may be reduced by as much as 50 percent. In addition to this, we should also see improved sales revenue through a reduction of lost sales.

QUESTIONS

1. What are the names of the two VICS CPFR® subcommittees for downstream collaboration?
2. Why is it more difficult to collaborate with downstream trading partners?
3. What is two-tier collaboration?
4. What is three-tier collaboration?
5. What does SRM mean?

13

ARE YOU READY FOR SUPPLY CHAIN COLLABORATION?

Hopefully by now, after you have read most of this book, you are convinced that supply chain collaboration is a good strategy for you and your company to implement or that you should expand your current trading partner collaborations. Supply chain collaboration should be looked at not as a question of "Should we do it?" but instead "When should we do it?" To help you decide on the "when," we have created a Supply Chain Collaboration Readiness Checklist to help highlight potential issues, opportunities, and gaps that you may wish to address prior to embarking on a collaborative supply chain program.

As we have said many times, internal collaboration is often harder than external collaboration. We suggest that you get your own house in order, as much as possible, prior to implementing a supply chain collaboration program with your trading partners. With this in mind, it is also a balance. You do not need to live in a perfect "Class A" internal world prior to engaging in a trading partner collaborative relationship. The financial benefits are so great that we do not believe you can afford to wait too long.

We all know that if we waited for the "perfect world" to become reality, we would never move forward, as we would always find some reason or excuse for not implementing supply chain collaboration. You need to assess your own risks and balance these risks prior to moving forward. We also want to caution you not to take on too much of a leap in company behavior and culture changes, but to build a roadmap of incremental steps that puts you on a path toward supply chain best practices. You will not need to be a Class A company to do supply chain collaboration, at least at first. Eventually, as you scale the collaboration effort, you will get better results as a company as you get closer to Class A behavior.

Oliver Wight International, Inc. first published *The Oliver Wight ABCD Checklist for Operational Excellence* in the 1970s and has continued to update the checklist through the years; a sixth edition is under preparation. The questions and criteria rankings were not compiled simply by one individual, but as a collection of experiences from hundreds of companies over a period of more than twenty-five years. Companies use this book to help identify where they currently are, based on these best-practice criteria, and to score themselves. Once companies have aligned their organizations to follow a best-practice direction, they can obtain the ultimate goal of achieving Class A status.

Our Supply Chain Collaboration Readiness Checklist is derived from the *ABCD Checklist for Operational Excellence* as well as from the outstanding effort of the VICS CPFR® Working Group that has created a CPFR® Readiness Assessment. Let's review the following supply chain collaborative checklist as you highlight for yourself your readiness for supply chain collaboration.

EXECUTIVE SPONSORSHIP

As we discussed before, a key lesson learned from the many companies that have already implemented supply chain collaboration programs was that executive-level sponsorship for the strategy is critical. This was a key finding because of the transformational nature and the significant organizational and cultural areas that can be impacted through such a program. Below are some basic "yes and no" questions you should consider to help make your supply chain collaboration program more of a success.

1. Do the company's senior executives understand the benefits of supply chain collaboration?
2. Have the executives received the necessary education and enlightenment in order to understand their personal roles as well as their functional roles and responsibilities in successful supply chain collaboration?
3. Is supply chain collaboration a part of the corporate strategic vision?
4. Has a financial cost/benefit analysis been performed to understand the financial benefits of collaboration?
5. Is there an executive-level sponsor for the supply chain collaboration process?

6. Are there competing initiatives for resources that could have an impact on the trading partner program?
7. Are all supply chain and corporate strategy functional areas involved in the supply chain collaboration program?
8. Do the company's senior executives understand that supply chain collaboration is an alignment of people, process, and technology that is internal as well as external?
9. Are the corporate executives aligned with the trading partner's executives?
10. Do the corporate executives have the vision and belief that supply chain collaboration can and should be a win/win partnership for everyone?

Scoring one point for each "yes" answer and zero for each "no" answer above, how did you do? If your total score was less than five points, you may want to work on getting more executive-level understanding and sponsorship prior to contacting a trading partner for a collaboration program.

SUPPLY CHAIN COLLABORATION CHECKLIST

Use the following to score the checklist:

4 = Excellent   3 = Very Good   2 = Fair   1 = Poor   0 = Not Doing

Culture	Best Practice	4	3	2	1	0
Empowerment	Employees are empowered with cross-functional metrics and incentives.	☐	☐	☐	☐	☐
Change Management	Speed to strategic transformations is considered critical. Priorities between tactical and strategic goals are balanced.	☐	☐	☐	☐	☐
Leadership	Totally committed to collaboration as a corporate strategic goal. Considers collaboration as one of the top priorities in the company.	☐	☐	☐	☐	☐
Internal Collaboration	Total enterprise has functional visibility. Functional areas understand individual contributions and relationship to team-wide benefits and goals.	☐	☐	☐	☐	☐
Project Focus	Proactive leadership — with a strong priority focus on transformational strategic initiatives.	☐	☐	☐	☐	☐

Process	Best Practice	4	3	2	1	0
Customer Collaboration	Customers communicate time-phased demand plans and schedules. As part of the joint business planning phase of collaboration, agreement is reached when customer-communicated plans represent a commitment to buy and when the plans are for general guidance.	☐	☐	☐	☐	☐
Sales Planning	The sales organization provides input that is fully integrated into the demand management process.	☐	☐	☐	☐	☐
Demand Management	The demand management process considers multiple views or inputs from sales, marketing, brand/product management, and customers. Consensus is reached on a demand plan each month and is integrated into the supply management process via sales and operations planning.	☐	☐	☐	☐	☐
Promotions and New Product Introductions	Collaborative planning is utilized in new product design and planning of promotions. Collaborative forecasting is leveraged with trading partners and internal resources.	☐	☐	☐	☐	☐
Supply Chain Management	Total integration of demand and supply chains is optimized in decision executions. Integration is achieved through sales and operations planning at the aggregate level for at least an eighteen-month planning horizon. Integration is also achieved through item-level demand-supply planning for the daily, weekly, and monthly planning horizons.	☐	☐	☐	☐	☐
Replenishment Processes	Processes exist that enable customer orders to flow through the planning system — from demand planning to order entry to supply planning. Demand planning is fully integrated with supply planning.	☐	☐	☐	☐	☐

Process	Best Practice	4	3	2	1	0
Metrics and Incentives	Functional and cross-functional metrics and incentives are in place. Balanced individual and team goals exist.	☐	☐	☐	☐	☐

Technology	Best Practice	4	3	2	1	0
Organization	Information technology is leveraged as a competitive advantage. A balance of purchased software with internal development is maintained. Understanding the business and speed to implementation is a critical requirement.	☐	☐	☐	☐	☐
Integration	The entire enterprise is completely integrated. Overlap of technology data is rare. Data can be found in one central area.	☐	☐	☐	☐	☐
Electronic Commerce	Ability to access supply chain information is made possible through electronic data interchange and private and public exchanges through two-way Internet communication.	☐	☐	☐	☐	☐
Automated Processing	Data and information are processed with little or no manual intervention. Exception-based reports are utilized for decision making, for balancing demand and supply, and inventory planning.	☐	☐	☐	☐	☐
Planning Tool Capabilities	Demand planning, supply chain planning, and collaboration software are used to enable collaboration with multiple trading partners. The software has the capability to manage demand and replenishment at store/item level. The forecasting and demand planning software is capable of communicating alerts when product forecasts exceed a maximum and minimum tolerance based on demand history.	☐	☐	☐	☐	☐

If your average score is less than "2," you should review some of the key areas of opportunity and assess where you may close the gap prior to implementing a supply chain collaboration program. We do not suggest that you jump from a "0 = not doing" to a "4 = excellent" in one swoop, as the risk of failure may be too great. Try to create a migration path of incremental steps to get you to the level of best practice you feel is good for your company.

You should also assess your readiness risks when it comes to a simple and more manual-intensive pilot process versus a fully automated production-scale supply chain collaboration effort. You may find that you can manage a simple pilot phase for supply chain collaboration, with little risk, without having best practices all in place, and the benefits of a successful pilot could provide you the corporate executive sponsorship that you will need later to get the support and financial funding for a more scalable rollout. For many companies, this bubbling-up process works well to prove to the executives, as well as the naysayers in a company, that the supply chain collaboration process is actually an important journey to embark on.

QUESTIONS

1. Why is it important to assess your collaboration readiness?
2. Do you have to be "Class A" before you start supply chain collaboration?
3. What are some of the key readiness leadership qualities that are needed?
    a. Why are these qualities important for collaboration?
4. Why is the technology readiness important?
    a. Piloting?
    b. Production?

14

ARE YOUR TRADING PARTNERS READY TO COLLABORATE?

Let's face it, not all of our trading partners are very collaborative. As we have said before, in many cases their definition of collaboration is: "I win; you figure out how to win." We have also seen trading partners, especially our customers, that do not even want to attempt to collaborate with a supplier as they look at everything as your problem and only focus on their own world. These closed-minded companies fail to look at the bigger picture of supply chain costs and inefficiencies and the impact on you rather than them. They fail to realize that the cost of goods sold often gets transferred right back to them in the long run. The companies just described are good examples of companies that you may not want to engage in a supply chain collaboration program. One industry analyst described this as "you can't teach a pig to sing."

You must pick your collaborative trading partners wisely and ensure that you minimize your risks of failure. Some keys points to remember about picking collaborative trading partners are:

- **Pick a strategic partner**, one that is important to you and your company. One rule of thumb is to collaborate by the 80/20 rule. Collaborate with the 20 percent of your trading partners with which you do 80 percent of your business.
- **Pick a trading partner that has already executed successful supply chain collaboration programs**. If the trading partner has already done

collaboration before and is committed to taking on new partners, your chance of success is fairly high. In addition, these partners may also have the collaboration templates for front-end arrangements in place, as well as the team structures and technology. Just as important, they will also have learned plenty of lessons.

■ **Pick a trading partner that believes in a win/win relationship.** We have observed some very successful supply chain collaborations when both trading partners want to obtain a "preferred trading partner" status. Typically, there is a one-sided "preferred vendor" status measurement with no accountability on the supply chain performance from the customer side. If both trading partners see the need to support and measure joint performance goals and scorecards, you have the potential for a winning combination.

SUPPLY CHAIN TRADING PARTNER READINESS CHECKLIST

We discussed your own internal readiness for supply chain collaboration in Chapter 13. We also created a simple list of readiness questions you should review concerning your trading partner's readiness to collaborate. You will need to assess your risk in going forward with these partnerships based on the answers to these questions. In addition, you will want to have your trading partner answer these same questions about your company. This, in itself, is an interesting exercise on joint alignment and understanding of each partner's capability and readiness.

1. Do the company's senior executives understand the benefits of trading partner collaboration?
2. Have the trading partner's executives received the necessary education and enlightenment in order to understand their personal roles as well as their functional roles and responsibilities in successful trading partner collaboration?
3. Is supply chain collaboration a part of the corporate strategic vision?
4. Has a financial cost/benefit analysis been performed to understand the financial benefits of collaboration?
5. Is there an executive-level sponsor for the supply chain collaboration?
6. Are there competing initiatives for resources at the trading partner that could have an impact on collaboration implementations?
7. Are all functional areas impacted by supply chain collaboration involved and supportive of the project?

8. Has the trading partner made a commitment to long-term partnerships?
9. Does the trading partner believe in a win/win relationship?
10. Has the trading partner been a participant in other supply chain collaboration efforts such as CPFR®?
11. Does the trading partner represent a significant portion of your business?
12. Have the technology investments been made to enable effective partnership programs?
13. Does the trading partner own collaborative software that is compliant with VICS CPFR®?
14. Is the collaboration software scalable to allow for forecast collaboration at the distribution center level or lower levels of detail?
15. Does the collaborated forecast integrate with execution systems?
16. Does a vendor scorecard exist that contains all key performance indicators and is it shared?
17. Do the company's senior executives understand that trading partner collaboration is not a technology solution, that the most successful implementations focus on people first, processes second, and technology third?
18. Are the trading partner's senior executives aligned with your own company's senior executives on the collaborative agreements and understandings necessary to support the collaborative partnership?
19. Do you trust your trading partner to keep information confidential?
20. Do you trust your trading partner to execute to what they collaborated on?

As with the checklist provided in the last chapter, score one point for each "yes" answer and zero points for each "no" answer. If you score less than ten points, then you might want to look at a different partner. In addition, in terms of the external trading partner's readiness for collaboration, you may also want to select certain critical questions as "no go" items. For example, if the trust criteria questions (19 and 20) are answered "no," we would consider those "no go" situations or, to put it in the words of the industry analyst, "That pig won't fly."

You may ask yourself how you can make the partnership stronger and more productive. What steps can you take to help the partnership develop into a win/win relationship? In many cases, this can be achieved by the alignment of the executives from the two companies in coming to a better understanding through an improved relationship. Other companies may evolve into collaborative partnerships through incentives such as revenue sharing on the performance improvements. This also may include performance deductions, which is much harder to get companies to agree to collaborate on. We have also seen some companies enable the customer trading partner to win first as the incentive for collaboration.

Whatever approach you take, make sure you perform the readiness risk assessment on the trading partner's willingness to collaborate in a best-practice manner. If you do not do this, you may just be using the same old methods, but using a more expensive approach. If you have a trading partner that will never satisfy the requirements of the majority of the readiness checklist, you may also want to assess the true value of the partnership. Is this pig not going to fly?

QUESTIONS

1. What are three reasons why a trading partner may not be a good collaborative trading partner?
2. What are three important qualifications for a trading partner's readiness to collaborate?
3. What questions are "no go" items when determining your trading partner's readiness to collaborate?

15

A PROVEN PATH
TO IMPLEMENTING
SUPPLY CHAIN
COLLABORATION

In the 1970s, the late Oliver Wight created what he called the "Proven Path." This roadmap of best-practice implementation steps has been a successful method of implementing the most complex of business process transformations as well as new technology. The Proven Path has been used for years for MRP II, ERP, sales and operations planning, and demand management implementations. Today, we are now using the same Proven Path for supply chain collaboration implementations.

METHODOLOGY

The Proven Path name comes from the fundamental fact that, if followed, it works. Implementing business excellence creates an opportunity to change the processes used to manage and operate the business. Success depends on the management of this change through the focused integration of people, processes, and technology. The Proven Path facilitates this change through its structured approach.

The Proven Path approach links improvement initiatives with business strategies and objectives so that your company achieves tangible, measurable op-

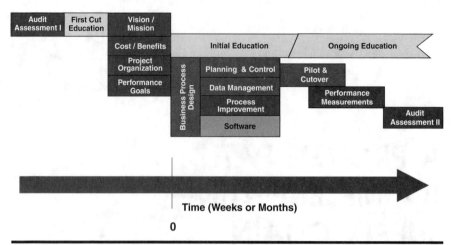

Figure 52.   Proven Path Methodology. (©2004 Oliver Wight International.)

erating results that contribute to profitability and competitive position. What makes this approach different from the traditional business process reengineering (BPR) approach is that it leverages off of a world-renowned set of business processes, behaviors, and metrics (*Class A*) that have been proven time and again to drive the types of results you seek.

The Proven Path approach reduces implementation risk while simultaneously delivering desired results by combining the power of the *ABCD Checklist for Operational Excellence* and the Supply Chain Collaboration Checklist (the what) with the power of the Proven Path (the how) to deliver sustainable, world-class results in the shortest space of time. The Proven Path is shown in Figure 52, and each step is described in detail below.

COMMITMENT PHASE

There are sixteen steps in the Proven Path. We call the first six the "pre-time-zero" steps. "Time zero" is that point in time when your company formally launches the project, that point in time when process redesign work commences.

The pre-time-zero steps are often referred to as the "commitment phase" of the initiative. Essential questions are posed and answered. What is it we are going to do? What is it going to take to do it (people, time, money...)? What do we expect to get in return for the investment of those resources? How will we measure success?

Deliverables from this phase normally include:

- An assessment of your starting position relative to industry best practices
- Leadership's understanding of supply chain collaboration concepts and principles
- A consensus-built, documented vision statement for this initiative
- A cost/benefit analysis resulting in a return on investment for this initiative
- A resource deployment plan for this initiative
- An agreement of which performance metrics are expected to improve and what levels they are expected to reach

ASSESSMENT

In order to formulate a detailed plan for success, you must first establish where you are starting from: where your company has pockets of excellence with management and operational processes and, more importantly, where voids and deficiencies exist in management and operational processes (see Figure 53).

To formally establish this starting point (point A), your company must appraise its current state. This first step is called an assessment. Some tools to assist you in the assessment are the checklists presented earlier.

The checklists include a series of questions, both overview and detailed in scope, that address the different processes and metrics used to manage and operate the business. The overview questions evaluate whether necessary operational and management processes exist and how well they are being employed. The detailed questions provide a means for assessing the significant

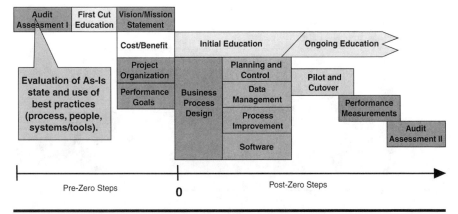

Figure 53. Audit/Assessment. (©2004 Oliver Wight International.)

characteristics of each process and, therefore, how effectively these processes are executed.

As we described earlier in the chapters on supply chain readiness, you will need to assess your current state, the potential gaps to close, and the risks of moving forward with collaboration and the risks of not moving forward. Once you have done the assessment, you can now move to the second step of the Proven Path.

FIRST-CUT EDUCATION

The leadership team needs to get a clear and common understanding of the elements of supply chain collaboration (see Figure 54). This is not education about computer systems, but rather about the management process as it impacts people and processes that is then supported by technology. Topics should include:

- What is supply chain collaboration?
- What are the benefits and risks?
- What have been some of the lessons learned from other companies that have implemented supply chain collaboration?
- What does it take to implement supply chain collaboration?
- What are the resources necessary for supply chain collaboration?
- What technology is required?
- What are the next steps we should take to get started in supply chain collaboration?

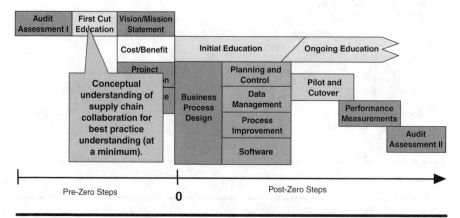

Figure 54. First Cut Education. (©2004 Oliver Wight International.)

On average, senior executive-level management can go through a high-level, first-cut education overview of supply chain collaboration in less than four hours. The middle management team needs a more substantial understanding of best-practice processes and behaviors since they will perform the detailed work involved during the implementation. These people typically need to attend, on average, a one-day course on supply chain collaboration. Depending on the company's situation determined in the assessment, additional education may be required before the next step. Supply chain collaboration must effectively integrate with other processes, like demand planning, sales and operations planning, and master scheduling, to achieve the optimum results. A common understanding of those processes is required by the management team as well.

VISION STATEMENT

The vision statement is one of the most important elements of the Proven Path. It is a high-level statement that defines the "what" of this initiative. As such, it provides the boundaries for all subsequent implementation activities (which develops the "how"). In short, it is the executives' specific direction for the implementation (see Figure 55).

This step of the Proven Path involves those who participated in the assessment and first-cut education work. By knowing where your company currently falls on the *Class A* scale and having a conceptual understanding of how *Class A* works, management will be sufficiently prepared to author this statement.

The important part of this activity is that management reaches *consensus* on where this initiative should take the business (matched expectations). It provides

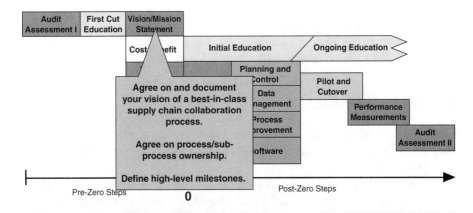

Figure 55.   Vision/Mission Statement. (©2004 Oliver Wight International.)

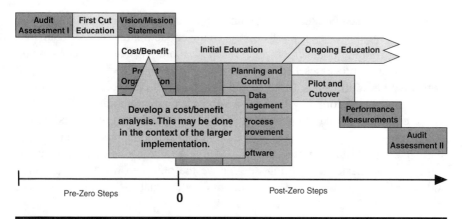

Figure 56. Cost/Benefit Analysis. (©2004 Oliver Wight International.)

for a common message with respect to these managers communicating the initiative to their departments and it facilitates consistent decision making downstream.

COST/BENEFIT ANALYSIS

As the vision statement is being completed, the members of the leadership team gain an appreciation for how the organization is currently operating versus the vision (see Figure 56). A plan of action must be developed and then implemented in order to achieve the stated vision. Part of this plan includes the development of implementation costs and anticipated benefits.

This comparison of costs and benefits will provide incentive for continuing the implementation. It will nurture a sense of ownership of the project and solidify leadership's commitment to allocating the requisite resources. If your people cannot make a sound business case from the results of this effort, the initiative should not be undertaken.

PROJECT ORGANIZATION

Leverage the project organization structures we described in Chapter 7 to create similar teams, from the executive-level steering committee to the project team (see Figure 57).

Every organization struggles to do what is necessary to change the business while simultaneously operating the business. However, for sustainable results, it is important that your company's people accomplish the bulk of the work.

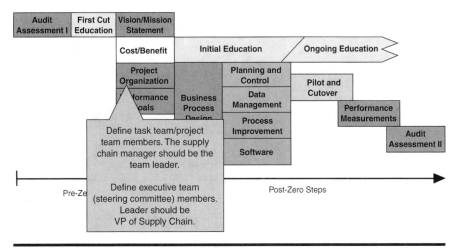

Figure 57. Project Organization. (©2004 Oliver Wight International.)

This builds understanding and ownership in the new processes. Consultants can provide assistance during your implementation, but they cannot and should not do it for you. Implementing best practices and performance improvements must be a self-improvement process. Consultants can guide you down the road, but your people are the ones who must generate the successes. Oliver Wight made a statement years ago that says it all: "It must be *your* blood on the bricks."

The project organization process starts by determining what actions must be completed to fill the gaps from the assessment and achieve the desired benefits. The project team assigns responsibilities, monitors the progress, and resolves issues throughout the implementation. A project team will shoulder the brunt of the work relative to the business process redesign activities (a post-time-zero step of the Proven Path). Spin-off task forces will be formed as needed. The assessment will determine where the gaps are; the spin-off task forces will be mobilized to go close those gaps.

PERFORMANCE GOALS

Class A recognition should not be the goal of this initiative. Excellent, integrated business processes and behaviors enabling the achievement of substantial *business results* should be the goal (see Figure 58).

Your company, no doubt, has already established performance measures, but additional ones may need to be established or current ones modified/deleted. It is important to delineate these measures and to monitor the progress toward

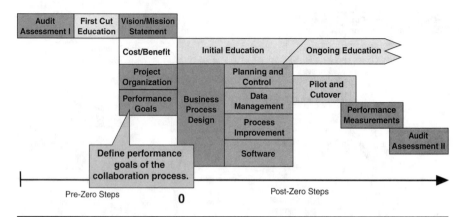

Figure 58.   Performance Goals. (©2004 Oliver Wight International.)

them throughout the implementation and thereafter. Accountability for the results must also be assigned and accepted by your company's leadership.

On completion of these pre-time-zero steps (commitment phase), leadership will have articulated the business case for moving forward and be in position to make a go/no-go decision. Assuming the business case is compelling, the implementation phase would begin. The next ten steps of the Proven Path are what we call the "post-time-zero" steps.

INITIAL EDUCATION

Initial education goes beyond first-cut education (see Figure 59). This education is designed to create "in-house experts" relative to best-practice processes consistent with your business process model pro-forma. This workshop-style education is very detailed and will enable process owners to participate in the process redesign effort that follows.

PROCESS DESIGN

Through a series of "business meetings," the project team (and invited key resources) will apply their learning from the prior steps of the Proven Path to develop the new reengineered business process blueprint (see Figure 60). It is also important to note that a separate and similar effort may be necessary with the selected collaborative trading partner(s) and joint collaborative business meetings to agree on the new trading partner collaborative business process blueprints.

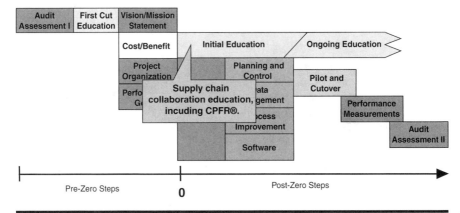

Figure 59. Initial Education. (©2004 Oliver Wight International.)

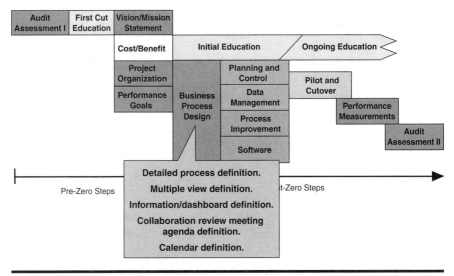

Figure 60. Business Process Design. (©2004 Oliver Wight International.)

PLANNING AND CONTROL

The new processes, collaborative agreements, and joint business plans need to be formally documented (see Figure 61). During this stage, your company policies, procedures, and measurements take full shape based on the new business collaborative process blueprint.

This process will be aligned with the trading partner's collaboration plans and controls, as well as expectations. All the planning and control processes will

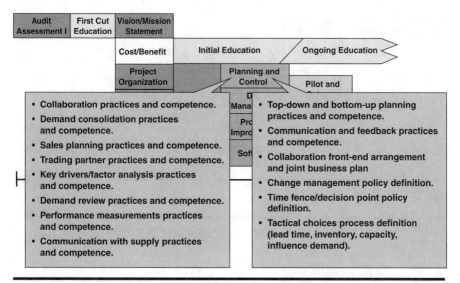

Figure 61. Planning and Control. (©2004 Oliver Wight International.)

be collectively reviewed for integration. Roles and responsibilities will be clearly defined. In some cases, one or more of the planning and control processes will be piloted (e.g., sales and operations planning) in order to shorten the time to results.

DATA MANAGEMENT

A key to success with an initiative such as this is the timeliness and accuracy of data (see Figure 62). Accountability and defined objectives will be assigned for all data elements. Where major work is required to clean up inaccurate data, this work will begin. Progress toward these data accuracy objectives will be reported regularly and will become part of the company's overall performance measurements.

PROCESS IMPROVEMENT

Throughout the life of the project, continuous improvement of all supply chain processes is essential. It should be decided which process improvements could be effectively accomplished in conjunction with this initiative and which must wait. Those process improvements deemed necessary to accomplish first will

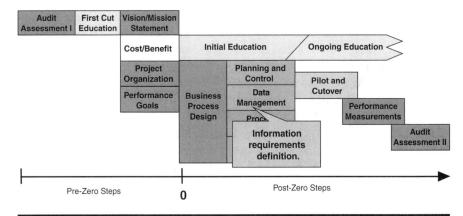

Figure 62.   Data Management. (©2004 Oliver Wight International.)

receive immediate attention as they will need to move forward with a sense of urgency.

SOFTWARE

You will need to assess your current technology capabilities and determine the gaps that will need to be closed at various stages of the supply chain collaboration program (see Figure 63). The overall intent should be to redesign the way

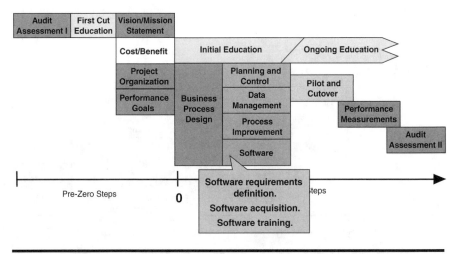

Figure 63.   Software Implementation. (©2004 Oliver Wight International.)

you manage and operate the business through the adoption of best-practice business processes and behaviors (otherwise, you will simply be "automating business as usual"). Only after doing so will you be in position to determine the best solution (hardware/software) to support the new environment.

Technology is a necessary part of supply chain collaboration, especially when it comes to scaling the collaborative efforts for multiple products and trading partners. Please note that process redesign is largely completed before applying the technology. As one company described the technology application: "You need to have common understanding, an agreed-upon process design, and then apply the technology. Stated differently, 'schools, rules and tools...in that order.'"

PILOT AND CUTOVER

Testing the collaboration process is essential (see Figure 64). Many lessons learned are obtained from the actual execution of the pilot process. One of the key lessons for a pilot is "not to eat the elephant," but to keep it simple so it will be easier to identify the lessons learned. The pilot process should be considered dynamic enough to be modified as required. What had been documented in the planning phases may need to be modified to support the business needs and the lessons learned during this collaborative pilot.

We typically suggest three pilots.

1. We suggest using minimal new technology for the first pilot as your first pilot should focus primarily on the people and process issues such as

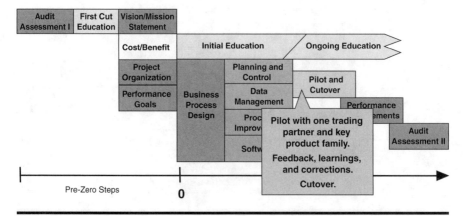

Figure 64. Pilot and Cutover. (©2004 Oliver Wight International.)

roles, responsibilities, accountabilities, and trust. If the pilot does not work, do not proceed without fixing the root cause of the failure. Was the issue people, processes, or technology? Fix it before moving on.

2. The second pilot should add collaborative technology as described in Chapter 8. This pilot will allow you to have a more scalable collaborative relationship and test the exception alert messages and the tolerance settings used to establish the alerts.

3. The third pilot should be a scalable pilot with the same trading partner, but with multiple product lines and functional areas involved.

PERFORMANCE MEASUREMENT

Key measurements will be targeted to improve effectiveness of internal processes, provide superior customer service, and enhance financial performance (see Figure 65). Actual results will be compared against previously established performance goals (a pre-time-zero step) to track progress.

Remember that some of these measures are business results measures. Are you improving in the areas you used to justify the project? Other measures will be process measures. Are the processes delivering the expected outcomes?

AUDIT/ASSESSMENT

Following successful cutover from the old to the new, an analysis of the company's new situation, problems, and opportunities will be performed (see

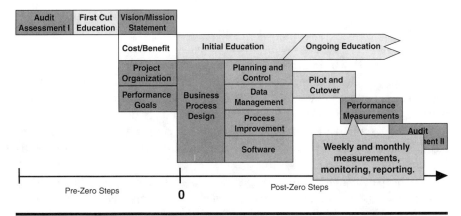

Figure 65. Performance Measurements. (©2004 Oliver Wight International.)

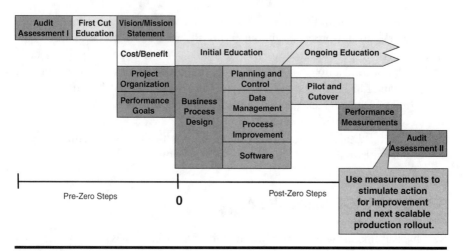

Figure 66. Audit/Assessment II. (©2004 Oliver Wight International.)

Figure 66). Verification of the effectiveness of the new tools and processes and a definition of continuous improvement steps will be performed. The outcome of this process will be a detailed plan (a roadmap) of your company's next steps on your continuous improvement journey.

ONGOING EDUCATION

A continuous improvement program demands a perennial effort to upgrade everyone's awareness and skill proficiency (see Figure 67). Ongoing education reinforces the initial education as well as acquaints new employees with the processes/behaviors/metrics/system. The performance measurement process will provide focus for ongoing education efforts.

Throughout the supply chain collaboration implementation, you and your trading partner(s) will possess absolute ownership of the process. The Proven Path focuses, aligns, and engages your entire organization with your company's and trading partner(s)' competitive priorities and turns fear of change into positive expectations. As a result, leaders and members both think and behave in ways that support the desired changes and immediately add more value to customers. Moreover, everyone is more flexible and adaptive as business realities continue to change.

As a separate note, many companies find that learning the Proven Path methodology is one of the surprising benefits of supply chain improvement initiatives. The effectiveness of a Proven Path implementation is something

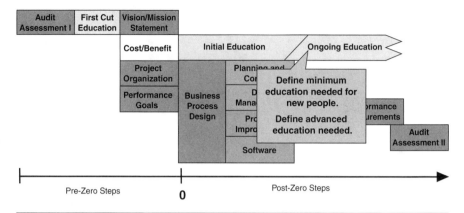

Figure 67. Ongoing Education. (©2004 Oliver Wight International.)

many people have not experienced before. It is applicable for the implementation of many different types of initiatives.

QUESTIONS

1. How many steps are in the Proven Path?
2. What are the Phase Zero steps?
3. Why is it important to have top management educated first on supply chain collaboration concepts?
4. How many pilots does the Proven Path suggest to have for supply chain collaboration at a minimum?
5. What are the key differences in the pilots?

16

SUPPLY CHAIN COLLABORATION: NEXT STEPS

Throughout this book, we have discussed why supply chain collaboration is important. We have provided you with examples of companies that have successfully implemented collaborative trading partnerships, the value and benefits that successful partnerships can provide, what technology is required for collaboration to occur, and methods for implementing supply chain collaboration programs for one or more partners.

The next step is up to you. From your observations in reading this book, do you see the value of exploring or expanding your efforts in supply chain collaboration? What sort of questions should you be asking yourself?

- Do you have a "bullwhip" effect in your supply chain?
- Do you find your company always in a reactive fire-fighting mode?
- Do you see product margins declining?
- Is forecasting accuracy an issue?
- Do you have excessive inventory and lead times?
- Are your customers demanding better customer service from you?
- Do you see your supply chain as the next competitive battlefield?
- Are your customers asking you to collaborate with them?
- Do you find yourself the "victim" of many of your customers' demands?
- Are your suppliers failing to perform to the levels you expect them to?

Chances are, you answered "yes" to most, if not all, of the questions above. This is true of most companies and why supply chain collaboration has become one of the leading supply chain best-practice initiatives any company can adopt.

Supply chain collaboration is a "transformational strategy," and it takes dedication, hard work, and commitment to execute. Supply chain collaboration, although not simple, is common sense.

At the May 2004 VICS CPFR® Working Group Meeting in Atlanta, Georgia, Andrew White, senior analyst for the Gartner Group, discussed a survey that was done on CPFR® adoption. He said that 46 percent of the respondents stated that CPFR® was too difficult to implement. But why is this? It is our belief that these respondents do not really understand what supply chain collaboration is and how they can successfully implement it based on their own company's readiness and trading partner's capabilities.

What are some of the key learnings discussed earlier in this book from supply chain collaboration partnerships that can help minimize the misunderstandings and complexity of implementing?

- Get educated on what supply chain collaboration is.
- Obtain executive sponsorship.
- Keep it simple.
- Collaborative arrangements are guidelines; one size does not fit all. Tailor the collaborative relationship to fit your needs and those of your trading partners.
- Pick a trading partner that wants to be in a win /win collaborative relationship.
- Understand the "value" potential that a good collaborative partnership can provide.
- Do not just study it, do it! Many lessons are learned by actually piloting, not by observing others piloting.

If you believe that supply chain collaboration is a good strategy for you and your company, then your next step should be to do it. If you have already implemented supply chain collaboration programs, then you should look at implementing with n-Tier suppliers and customers, expanding the number of products to collaborative processes, and expanding on overall collaborative planning processing.

If you have not done a formalized, collaborative program with a trading partner, then structure and start a simple pilot based on the information provided in this book. Be a participant, not an observer. Do not allow yourself to be caught in the "excuse" mode for not doing something about it.

Supply chain collaboration is not going away. We see this process permeating all industries globally. It may have different names, such as supplier relationship management, CPFR®, RossettaNet, trading partner collaboration, customer relationship management, sales and operations planning, and supply chain collaboration, but regardless of what it is called, it is a "no brainer" that you should leverage your internal as well as external supply chain partners to work together for the benefit of the entire supply chain. Collaborative orchestration is the goal. Implementing is mandatory.

QUESTIONS

1. What are three issues you see where supply chain collaboration would help your company?
2. What are three key learnings that were discussed in this book?

APPENDIX:
SAMPLE FRONT-END
AGREEMENT

TRADING PARTNERS

- ABC Stores, Inc.
- XYZ Manufacturing Co., Inc.

I. CPFR AGREEMENT AND STATEMENT

A. Purpose

ABC STORES and XYZ MFG agree to collaborate in key supply chain processes using standards developed by the Voluntary Interindustry Commerce Standards (VICS) Association called Collaborative Planning, Forecasting, and Replenishment (CPFR®). Our goal is to increase mutual efficiencies and delight the end consumer through dynamic information sharing, focus on common goals and measures, and commit to the CPFR® processes. We recognize that there are many business process, technological, and organizational *changes* required by this collaboration, and we commit to apply resources to make these changes in order to make our collaboration effective and meet our mutual goals.

B. Confidentiality

All communication will be governed by antitrust regulations. Both trading partners commit here to absolute confidentiality in the use of information shared.

CPFR ©1998, Voluntary Interindustry Commerce Standards (VICS) Association.

II. CPFR GOALS AND OBJECTIVES

A. Opportunity

Through CPFR®, ABC STORES and XYZ MFG will seek to reduce out-of-stocks, increase sales, reduce business transaction costs, improve the use of capital (especially that involved in inventory), and facilitate trading partner relationships.

B. Measurement of Success

ABC STORES and XYZ MFG agree to focus on key results-oriented measures: retail in stock, inventory turns (at retail), and forecast accuracy (measured when the forecast can impact production, eight weeks prior). Goals for specific products are attached, but the *overall* goal is 96 percent retail in stock, six turns at retail, <15 percent sales forecast error (eight weeks out), and <20 percent order forecast error (eight weeks out). We also agree to maintain several measures involving performance of specific parts of the process. Our performance against all of these measures will be the basis of our quarterly face-to-face reviews. Details on these measures (scope, data source, responsibility for maintaining, frequency of measure, frequency of reporting, construction of the algorithm, unit of measure) will be attached to this agreement.

- Supporting processes are detailed in the process models (to be attached).

III. DISCUSSION OF COMPETENCIES, RESOURCES, AND SYSTEMS

Based on our earlier discussion of the competencies, resources, and systems that each party brings to the partnership, we agree to follow the CPFR® Scenario B where the retailer has the ultimate responsibility for the sales forecast, the manufacturer has ultimate responsibility for the order forecast, and the manufacturer has ultimate responsibility for order generation.

IV. DEFINITION OF COLLABORATION POINTS AND RESPONSIBLE BUSINESS FUNCTIONS

A. Collaboration Points

Collaboration points include the joint business plan, the sales forecast, and the order forecast. Collaboration on the sales and order forecast will be driven by the following item-level exception criteria and values:

- **Sales forecast exception criteria** — Retail in stock <95 percent, sales forecast error >20 percent, sales forecast differs from same week prior year >10 percent, change in promotional calendar or number of active stores
- **Order forecast exception criteria** — Retail in stock < 95 percent, order forecast error >20 percent, annualized retail turns < goal (as noted on item management profile table), entry of new event that impacts inventory/orders, emergency orders requested >5 percent of weekly forecast

B. Responsible Business Functions

The following business functional units are impacted by and responsible for the success of CPFR®:

- Retailer: merchandising/buying, forecasting, inventory management
- Manufacturer: sales team, planning/forecasting, distribution

V. INFORMATION SHARING NEEDS

Information sharing will be open and routine as needed to support CPFR® processes. No information on competitor activity will be shared. As it is our expectation that communication will be timely, the collaboration information cycle time will be measured.

A. Areas of Information Sharing

- Data necessary to *measure success* (common metrics) such as retail in-stock percent, inventory, and forecast accuracy
- Data necessary to *identify exceptions* in the sales and order forecast such as retail in-stock percent, inventory turns and levels (retail, in transit, warehouse), sales and order forecast accuracy, vendor order fill rate, etc.
- Data necessary to *support decisions about exception items* such as promotions, planned inventory actions and other events that impact the forecast, point-of-sale data, historical shipments, sales and order forecasts, current item in-stock percent retail, current inventory turns, number of valid stores, etc.
- Item management profile including item identifiers, logistics rules (rounding rules, order minimum and multiples, configurations, etc.)
- Complete details are listed in the data model (to be attached)

B. Frequency of Updates

Forecasts will be created and shared on a weekly basis. Exceptions, supporting data, and item management data will be shared daily, and metrics will be calculated and shared monthly.

C. Method of Data Sharing

Where possible, data sharing will be accomplished using standard data formats such as EDI transaction sets. This includes, but is not limited to, VICS EDI 830 (planning schedule with release capability), VICS EDI 832 (price/sales catalog), VICS EDI 850 (purchase order), VICS EDI 852 (product activity data), VICS EDI 855 (purchase order acknowledgment), and VICS EDI 856 (ship notice/manifest).

D. Recovery and Response Times

Response time for the CPFR® system used by ABC STORES and XYZ MFG should be no more than thirty seconds. Steps have been taken to limit recovery time following a system fault to twelve hours.

VI. SERVICE AND ORDERING COMMITMENTS

One of the ways both companies expect to benefit from forecast collaboration is through commitments to supply the forecast and to consume the forecast through orders (subject to a range of deviation). The range of deviation will be re-evaluated periodically. XYZ MFG agrees to support the agreed to forecast (at a frozen period of seven days) with timely shipments within 3 percent of the forecast (measured weekly). In return, ABC STORES agrees to consume the forecast through orders within 3 percent (measured weekly). In the event that these limits will be exceeded, the respective party will notify the other as soon as possible and will determine a resolution plan. In recognition of the spirit of this agreement, both parties agree to commit the resources and systems necessary to maintain the "upstream" planning processes, which will in turn allow the timely identification and resolution of potential issues.

VII. RESOURCE INVOLVEMENT AND COMMITMENTS

The following specific resources and activities have been determined to be necessary for successful collaboration.

	Key Participants		
Process	**ABC Stores**	**XYZ Mfg**	**Activities**
Joint Business Planning	Category buyer and planner	Sales team manager and analyst, category manager	Category buyer and planner meet with the sales team manager, analyst, or category manager quarterly to develop the joint business plan as defined in the process model. Participants share responsibility for outputs: the joint business plan and the item management profile.
Sales Forecasting	Category buyer and planner, forecasting analyst, new store planner	Sales team manager and analyst	Based on joint business plan and other inputs (POS data, events, causal information), ABC forecasting analyst creates the sales forecast weekly. The following are responsible for input that drives the forecast: ABC category buyer, planner, and new store planner and the XYZ sales team manager and analyst (responsible for maintaining events and communicating the joint business plan). The ABC category planner and the XYZ sales analyst are responsible for initiating the resolution of exception items.
Order Forecasting	Category buyer and planner, forecasting analyst, inventory rebuyer, logistics planner	Sales team manager and analyst, forecasting manager	Based on the sales forecast, order forecast impact events, inventory strategies, and current inventory position, the XYZ sales team analyst and forecasting manager create the order forecast weekly. The following are responsible for input that drives the forecast: ABC category buyer and planner, forecasting analyst, inventory rebuyer, and logistics planner, XYZ sales team manager, analyst, and forecasting manager. The ABC category planner and the XYZ sales analyst are responsible for initiating the resolution of exception items.
Order Generation	Category buyer	Inventory planner	Based on the frozen period of the order forecast, the XYZ inventory planner generates orders. The need to generate orders is evaluated daily.

VIII. RESOLUTION OF CPFR® DISAGREEMENTS

In the event of a CPFR® disagreement, the ultimate process owners will have final say over the sales forecast, order forecast, and order generation if intermediate efforts at resolution are not successful. All other disagreements will be handled by a meeting of the leaders of the affected functional areas, and ultimately the CPFR® agreement owners.

IX. CPFR® AGREEMENTS REVIEW CYCLE

This agreement will be reviewed each year in January, and the undersigned will reaffirm the effectiveness of the process by renewing the agreement.

X. SIGNATURES

- VP, Merchandising, ABC Stores
- VP, Logistics, ABC Stores
- President, XYZ Manufacturing
- VP, Customer Team, XYZ Manufacturing

INDEX